ORDINARY LANGUAGE

Essays in Philosophical Method

Edited by

V. C. CHAPPELL

Dover Publications, Inc.
New York

Published in Canada by General Publishing Company,
Ltd., 30 Lesmill Road, Don Mills, Toronto, Ontario.
Published in the United Kingdom by Constable and Com-
pany, Ltd., 10 Orange Street, London WC2H 7EG.

This Dover edition, first published in 1981, is an unabridged
republication of the work originally published in 1964 by
Prentice-Hall, Inc., Englewood Cliffs, N.J., as part of the
series *Contemporary Perspectives in Philosophy.* The general
introduction by the series editors, Joel Feinberg and Wesley C.
Salmon, has been omitted from this edition.

International Standard Book Number: 0-486-24082-7
Library of Congress Catalog Card Number: 80-69248

Manufactured in the United States of America
Dover Publications, Inc.
180 Varick Street
New York, N.Y. 10014

CONTENTS

ORDINARY LANGUAGE

Essays in Philosophical Method

INTRODUCTION

V. C. CHAPPELL

Preoccupation with language has been a distinctive feature of twentieth-century philosophy. Interest in language as such, of course, is nothing new; philosophers have studied it, as one subject among others, since the time of the Greeks. What is new is the study of language in order to achieve results on other subjects—mind, morals, nature, even God. The idea is that language can be made to yield truths about such subjects, or at least solutions to problems concerning them, as well as about itself. Among the first to formulate this idea and put it into philosophical practice were Frege and Russell around the turn of the century. G. E. Moore helped to promote it by his method of philosophizing, though he disclaimed any interest in language as such. The most influential proponent of this linguistic conception of philosophy, however, was Wittgenstein. First with his *Tractatus,* published in England in 1922, and then through his teaching at Cambridge in the Thirties and Forties, Wittgenstein converted large numbers of philosophers to the view that philosophy is essentially linguistic. It is in large

1

part owing to his work that this view is dominant in Anglo-American philosophy today.

There are, however, two quite different versions of this view, corresponding roughly to the two quite different ways in which Wittgenstein himself conceived philosophy and language in the *Tractatus* and in his later work. The one version, deriving in part from the *Tractatus* and promoted by the logical positivists, turns about the notion of an ideal language. The premise here is that ordinary language is somehow deficient or faulty, at least for philosophical purposes, and that philosophical success—clarification and the dissolution of problems—is to be achieved by constructing a logically perfect language with which to replace it. The other version derives in large part from Wittgenstein's own repudiation of this premise in his teaching after 1930. Here the conviction is that "ordinary language is all right," and that philosophical difficulties, which are indeed linguistic in origin, arise not because our language is faulty but because philosophers misdescribe and misconstrue it. It follows that the way to achieve success in philosophy—and this again means understanding and the solving of problems—is to determine how our language is in fact used, and thence show where and how philosophers have gone astray. It is this latter version of the linguistic conception of philosophy to which the term "ordinary language philosophy" has been applied, and which is the concern of the essays collected in the present volume.

Ordinary language philosophy has been practiced by two main philosophical groups, though neither group constitutes an organized "school." The first comprises those philosophers who were influenced more or less directly by Wittgenstein himself. Here the chief figures are Wisdom, Malcolm, Waismann, Anscombe, Bouwsma, and Lazerowitz. The work of this group is represented in this volume by Malcolm's paper on the philosophical method of Moore. Malcolm interprets the philosophizing of both Moore's opponents and Moore himself along Wittgensteinian lines, arguing that the philosophical claims in both cases are essentially claims about language, the former violating or rejecting and the latter defending our ordinary ways of speaking. Moore is the victor in these contests, Malcolm contends, because "ordinary language is correct language." Malcolm may or may not be right in his interpretation of Moore—and Moore himself rejected this account of his philosophical procedure—and he certainly overstates his case. But his paper is valuable for its clear presentation and plausible defense of the Wittgensteinian view that philosophical problems are linguistic in character and are to be solved by appealing to the ordinary use of the expressions on which they turn.

The other main group of ordinary language philosophers is that which grew up at Oxford just after the war, under the leadership first of Ryle and later of Austin. Its most distinguished members, after Ryle and Austin, are Strawson, Hart, Hampshire, Hare, Urmson, and War-nock; and a host of others, at Oxford and elsewhere, have followed the Oxford line. Comparisons are hard, but it may be said in general that the Oxford philosophers tend to be more interested in the actual details of ordinary language and in drawing general philosophical conclu-sions than the Wittgensteinians, who tend to restrict themselves to the solution of specific problems. Austin carried the attitude of disinterested curiosity about the workings of language farther than anybody, and he himself foresaw the eventual absorption of his sort of enterprise in an expanded science of linguistics.

The work of the Oxford philosophers and the Wittgensteinians alike has aroused much criticism in the course of its rise to prominence in Anglo-American philosophy. Malcolm's Moore paper was roundly at-tacked soon after it appeared, as were such early Oxford works as Ryle's *Concept of Mind*. What was attacked was not so much the specific results of the ordinary language philosophers as their underlying con-ceptions of philosophy and of language—the linguistic conception of philosophy and the notion of ordinary language as a philosophical touch-stone. Many of the attacks were based on misunderstanding; others raised legitimate and pertinent philosophical questions. For the most part, however, the ordinary language philosophers avoided general methodological discussions and stuck to their job of producing particular results. Most of the criticism of their work, therefore, went unanswered, though it seemed clear that both explanation and defense of their pro-cedures were necessary. One major exception to this trend among the Oxford philosophers was Ryle, who in his paper on "Ordinary Lan-guage," included in this volume, tried to remove some of the more persistent misunderstandings that had arisen over the notion of ordinary language and the practice of ordinary language philosophy. Another was Austin in his paper on "Excuses," also included here, which con-tains the most authoritative and compelling description on record by an Oxford philosopher of his philosophical method.

Neither Ryle nor Austin, however, succeeded in satisfying the more determined critics of ordinary language philosophy. Ryle's own account of ordinary language was questioned and Austin's statement was too brief to answer some of the harder questions which began to be posed. Chief among these was that raised by Benson Mates in his symposium with Stanley Cavell, the question of "the verification of statements about ordinary language." How does one know what language is ordinary, or when a use of an expression is an ordinary use, or how to settle disputes between those who disagree about a point of language? Mates claimed that these questions had not been satisfactorily answered by ordinary language philosophers, and Cavell, in his reply to Mates's paper, undertook to answer them, and others besides. His long paper, included here with Mates's, is the most detailed explanation and defense of the procedures of the ordinary language philosophers that has yet appeared.

Cavell has himself been attacked in a recent paper by Fodor and Katz (*see* Bibliography), who have also mounted a new and more serious attack on ordinary language philosophy generally, chiefly on the grounds that its practitioners pretend to do informally and nonempirically what only can be done, in their opinion, by the trained masters of empirical linguistics. The recent development of linguistic science, they argue, has made ordinary language philosophy obsolete. It is nonetheless an open question at the present time whether these and other attacks are finally justified and whether ordinary language philosophy has indeed run its course. But there can be no doubt of its immense influence in recent philosophical thought and of its permanent contribution to the progress of philosophy.

The papers in this volume have all been previously published and are reprinted by permission of their authors and the editors of the journals or books in which they first appeared. Specific acknowledgment is given at the beginning of each paper. Cavell's paper has been slightly altered for its republication here; the others have all been reprinted as they first appeared, except that obvious mistakes have been corrected, footnotes renumbered, references filled out, and spelling revised to accord with current American usage. Cross-references within papers to others included in this volume are all to pages of this volume.

MOORE AND

ORDINARY LANGUAGE

NORMAN MALCOLM

I

In this paper I am going to talk about an important feature of Professor Moore's philosophical method, namely, his way of refuting a certain type of philosophical proposition.

I shall begin by giving a list of propositions all of which have been maintained or are now maintained by various philosophers. Every one of these statements would, I am sure, be rejected by Moore as false. Furthermore, if with regard to each of these statements, he were asked to give a *reason* for rejecting that statement, or were asked to *prove* it to be false, he would give a *reason* or *proof* which would be strikingly similar in the case of each statement. I want to examine the general character of this common method of proof in order to show the point

From The Philosophy of G. E. Moore, *Paul Arthur Schilpp, ed. (Evanston, Ill.: The Library of Living Philosophers, Inc., 1942). Reprinted by permission of the author, the editor, and The Library of Living Philosophers, Inc.*

and the justification of it. I think that showing the point and the justification of Moore's method of attacking this type of philosophical statement will throw great light on the nature of philosophy, and also explain Moore's importance in the history of philosophy.

The following is my list of philosophical statements:

1. There are no material things.
2. Time is unreal.
3. Space is unreal.
4. No one ever perceives a material thing.
5. No material thing exists unperceived.
6. All that one ever sees when he looks at a thing is part of his own brain.
7. There are no other minds—my sensations are the only sensations that exist.
8. We do not know for *certain* that there are any other minds.
9. We do not know for *certain* that the world was not created five minutes ago.
10. We do not know for *certain* the truth of any statement about material things.
11. All empirical statements are hypotheses.
12. A priori statements are rules of grammar.

Let us now consider Moore's way of attacking these statements. With regard to each of them I am going to state the sort of argument against it which I think Moore would give, or at least which he would approve.

1. Philosopher: "There are no material things."

Moore: "You are certainly wrong, for here's one hand and here's another; and so there are at least two material things." [1]

2. Philosopher: "Time is unreal."

Moore: "If you mean that no event ever follows or precedes another event, you are certainly wrong; for *after* lunch I went for a walk, and after that I took a bath, and after that I had tea." [2]

3. Philosopher: "Space is unreal."

Moore: "If you mean that nothing is ever to the right of, or to the left of, or behind, or above anything else, then you are certainly wrong; for this inkwell is to the left of this pen, and my head is above them both."

4. Philosopher: "No one ever perceives a material thing." [3]

---

[1] See Moore, "Proof of an External World," *Proceedings of the British Academy,* Vol. XXV (1939); reprinted in Moore, *Philosophical Papers* (London: George Allen & Unwin, 1959).

[2] See Moore, "The Conception of Reality," *Philosophical Studies* (London: Routledge & Kegan Paul, Ltd., 1922), pp. 209ff.

[3] This is the philosopher who says that all we really perceive are sense-data, and that sense-data are not material things, nor parts of material things.

Moore: "If by 'perceive' you mean 'hear,' 'see,' 'feel,' etc., then nothing could be more false; for I now both see and feel this piece of chalk."

5. Philosopher: "No material thing exists unperceived."

Moore: "What you say is absurd, for no one perceived my bedroom while I was asleep last night and yet it certainly did not cease to exist."

6. Philosopher: "All that one ever sees when one looks at a thing is part of one's own brain." [4]

Moore: "This desk which both of us now see is most certainly not part of my brain, and, in fact, I have never seen a part of my own brain."

7. Philosopher: "How would you prove that the statement that your own sensations, feelings, experiences are the only ones that exist is false?"

Moore: "In this way: I know that *you* now see me and hear me, and furthermore I know that my wife has a toothache, and therefore it follows that sensations, feelings, experiences other than my own exist."

8. Philosopher: "You do not know for *certain* that there are any feelings or experiences other than your own."

Moore: "On the contrary, I know it to be *absolutely* certain that you now see me and hear what I say, and it is absolutely certain that my wife has a toothache. Therefore, I do know it to be absolutely certain that there exist feelings and experiences other than my own."

9. Philosopher: "We do not know for certain that the world was not created five minutes ago, complete with fossils." [5]

Moore: "I know for certain that I and many other people have lived for many years, and that many other people lived many years before us; and it would be absurd to deny it."

10. Philosopher: "We do not know for certain the truth of any statement about material things."

Moore: "Both of us know for *certain* that there are several chairs in this room, and how absurd it would be to suggest that we do not know it, but only believe it, and that perhaps it is not the case!"

11. Philosopher: "All empirical statements are really hypotheses."

Moore: "The statement that I had breakfast an hour ago is certainly an empirical statement, and it would be ridiculous to call it an hypothesis."

12. Philosopher: "A priori statements are really rules of grammar."

Moore: "That 6 times 9 equals 54 is an a priori statement, but it is most certainly wrong to call it a rule of grammar."

---

[4] "I should say that what the physiologist sees when he looks at a brain is part of his own brain, not part of the brain he is examining." Bertrand Russell, *The Analysis of Matter* (London: George Allen & Unwin, 1927), p. 383.

[5] Cf. Russell, *An Outline of Philosophy* (London: George Allen & Unwin, 1927), p. 7. This is a way of expressing the view that no statements about the *past* are known with certainty.

It is important to notice that a feature which is common to all of the philosophical statements in our list is that they are *paradoxical*. That is, they are one and all statements which a philosophically unsophisticated person would find shocking. They go against "common sense." This fact plays an important part in the explanation of the nature of Moore's attacks upon these statements.

Let us examine the general nature of Moore's refutations. There is an inclination to say that they one and all *beg the question*. When the philosopher said that a priori statements are rules of grammar he meant to include the statement that 6 times 9 equals 54 among a priori statements. He meant to say of *it,* as well as of every other a priori statement, that it really is a rule of grammar. When Moore simply denies that it is a rule of grammar, he seems to beg the question. At least his reply does not seem to be a fruitful one; it does not seem to be one which ought to convince the philosopher that what he said was false.

When the philosopher says that there are no material things, is it not the case that part of what he means is that there are no hands; or, if he would allow that there are hands, part of what he means is that hands are not material things? So that Moore's refutation, which asserts of two things that they are hands, and asserts that hands are material things, in one way or another begs the question.

And when the philosopher says that one does not know for certain that there are any sensations, feelings, experiences other than one's own, part of what he means to say is that one never knows for certain that one's wife has a toothache; and when Moore insists that he does know for certain that his wife has a toothache, he begs the question. At least it seems a poor sort of refutation; not one which ought to convince any philosopher that what he said was wrong.

I hold that what Moore says in reply to the philosophical statements in our list is in each case perfectly true; and furthermore, I wish to maintain that what he says is in each case a *good* refutation, a refutation that shows the falsity of the statement in question. To explain this is the main purpose of my paper.

The essence of Moore's technique of refuting philosophical statements consists in pointing out that these statements *go against ordinary language*. We need to consider, first, in what way these statements do go against ordinary language; and, second, how does it refute a philosophical statement to show that it goes against ordinary language?

When Russell said that what the physiologist sees when he looks at a brain is part of his own brain, not part of the brain he is examining, he was of course not referring to any particular physiologist, but to all physiologists, and not only to all physiologists, but to every person whomsoever. What he meant to imply was that whenever in the past a person has said that he sees a tree or a rock or a piece of cheese on the table, what he has said was really false; and that whenever in the future any person will say that he sees a house or a car or a rabbit, what he will say really will be false. All that will ever really be true *in any case whatever* in which a person says that he sees something will be that he sees a part of his own brain.

Russell's statement is a most startling one. Nothing could be more paradoxical! And what sort of a statement is it? Did Russell mean to imply that whenever in the past any physiologist has thought that he was seeing someone else's brain he has been *deceived?* Suppose that, unknown to the physiologist, a section of his cranium had been removed and furthermore there was, also unknown to him, an ingenious arrangement of mirrors, such that when he tried to look at a brain in front of him, what he actually saw was a part of his own brain in his own skull. Did Russell mean to say that this is the sort of thing which has always happened in the past when a physiologist has tried to examine a brain, and which will always happen in the future? If he were making this straight-forward empirical statement, then it is clear that he would have no evidence whatever for it. It is not the sort of empirical statement that an intelligent man would make.

No, Russell was not making an empirical statement. In the normal sort of circumstances in which a person would ordinarily say that he sees the postman, Russell would agree with him as to what the particular circumstances of the situation were. Russell would not disagree with him about any question of empirical fact; yet Russell would still say that what he really saw was not the postman, but part of his own brain. It appears then that they disagree, not about any empirical facts, but about what *language* shall be used to describe those facts. Russell was saying that it is really *a more correct way of speaking* to say that you see a part of your brain, than to say that you see the postman.

The philosophical statement "All that one ever sees when one looks at a thing is part of one's brain" may be interpreted as meaning "Whenever one looks at a thing, it is really more correct language to say that one sees a part of one's brain than to say that one sees the thing in question." And Moore's reply, "This desk which both of us see is not a part of my brain," may be interpreted as meaning "It is correct language to say that what we are doing now is seeing a desk, and it is not correct language to say that what we are doing now is seeing parts of our brains." [6]

---

[6] It must not be assumed that Professor Moore would agree with my interpretation of the nature of the philosophical paradoxes, nor with my interpretation of the nature of his refutations of those paradoxes. That Moore does employ such refutations anyone knows who is familiar with his language and discussions. But this paper's analysis of the philosophical paradoxes and of Moore's refutations is not one that Moore has ever suggested.

When the dispute is seen in this light, then it is perfectly clear that Moore is right. We can see that the philosophical statement which he is attacking is false, no matter what arguments may be advanced in favor of it.[7] The "proofs" of it may be ever so tempting, but we are right in rejecting them as false statements without even examining them. For it is obvious to us upon the slightest reflection that a person may wish to see the Empire State building; and that a way in which we might describe in ordinary language what happened when he fulfilled his wish would be by saying the words "He is now seeing the Empire State building for the first time"; and that we would never accept as a correct description of what happened the words "He is now seeing a part of his brain." What Moore's reply reminds us of is that situations constantly occur which ordinary language allows us to describe by uttering sentences of the sort "I see my pen," "I see a cat," etc. and which it would be outrageously incorrect to describe by saying "I see a part of my brain." It is in this way that Moore's reply constitutes a refutation of the philosophical statement.

Let us consider the philosophical statement "We do not know for *certain* the truth of any statement about material things," and Moore's typical sort of reply, "Both of us know for *certain* that there are several chairs in this room, and how absurd it would be to suggest that we do not know it, but only believe it, and that perhaps it is not the case— how absurd it would be to say that it is highly probable, but not certain!" The view that we do not know for certain the truth of any statement about material things, and the wider view that we do not know for certain the truth of *any* empirical statement, are very popular views among philosophers.[8] Let us notice how sweeping and how paradoxical is the philosopher's statement that we never know for certain that any statement about material things is true.

In ordinary life everyone of us has known of particular cases in

---

[7] What led Russell to make the statement was his being led to the view (1) that what we really see are "percepts": and (2) that each person's "percepts" are located in that person's brain. Neither of these statements expresses an empirical proposition.

[8] E.g., ". . . all empirical knowledge is probable only." C. I. Lewis, *Mind and the World-Order* (New York: Charles Scribner's Sons, 1929), p. 309; "We have . . . found reason to doubt external perception, in the full-blooded sense in which common-sense accepts it." Russell, *An Outline of Philosophy, op. cit.*, p. 10; ". . . We can never be completely certain that any given proposition is true. . . ." Russell, *An Inquiry into Meaning and Truth* (London: George Allen & Unwin, 1940), p. 166; ". . . No genuine synthetic proposition . . . can be absolutely certain." A. J. Ayer, *Language, Truth, and Logic* (London: Oxford University Press, 1936), p. 127; ". . . Statements about material things are not conclusively verifiable." Ayer, *The Foundations of Empirical Knowledge* (London: Macmillan & Co., Ltd., 1940), p. 239.

which a person has said that he knew for certain that some material-thing statement was true, but that it has turned out that he was mistaken. Someone may have said, for example, that he knew for certain by the smell that it was carrots that were cooking on the stove. But you had just previously lifted the cover and seen that it was turnips, not carrots. You are able to say, *on empirical grounds,* that *in this particular case* when the person said that he knew for certain that a material-thing statement was true, he was mistaken. Or you might have known that it was wrong of him to say that he knew for certain it was carrots, not because you had lifted the cover and seen the turnips, but because you knew from past experience that cooking carrots smell like cooking turnips, and so knew that he was not entitled to conclude from the smell alone that it was *certain* that it was carrots. It is an empirical fact that *sometimes* when people use statements of the form: "I know for certain that p," where p is a material-thing statement, what they say is false.

But when the philosopher asserts that we never know for certain *any* material-thing statements, he is not asserting this empirical fact. He is asserting that *always* in the past when a person has said "I know for certain that p," where p is a material-thing statement, he has said something false. And he is asserting that *always* in the future when any person says a thing of that sort his statement will be false. The philosopher says that this is the case no matter what material-thing statement is referred to, no matter what the particular circumstances of the case, no matter what evidence the person has in his possession! If the philosopher's statement were an empirical statement, we can see how absurdly unreasonable it would be of him to make it—far more unreasonable than it would be of a man, who knew nothing about elephants, to say that an elephant never drinks more than a gallon of water a day.

The philosopher does not commit *that* sort of absurdity, because his statement is not an empirical one. The reason he can be so cocksure, and not on empirical grounds, that it never has been and never will be right for any person to say "I know for certain that p," where p is a material-thing statement, is that he regards that *form of speech* as *improper.* He regards it as improper in just the same way that the sentence "I see something which is totally invisible" is improper. He regards it as improper in the sense in which every self-contradictory expression is improper. Just as it would never be proper for you to describe *any* experience of yours by saying "I see something which is totally invisible," so the philosopher thinks that it would never be proper for you to describe any state of affairs by saying "I know for certain that p," where p is a material-thing statement.

Among the philosophers who maintain that no material-thing statement can be certain, Mr. Ayer is one who realizes that when he makes this statement he is not making an empirical judgment, but is condemning a certain form of expression as improper. He says,

> We do indeed verify many such propositions [i.e., propositions which imply the existence of material things] to an extent that makes it highly probable that they are true; but since the series of relevant tests, being infinite, can never be exhausted, this probability can never amount to logical certainty. . . .
>
> It must be admitted then that there is a sense in which it is true to say that we can never be sure, with regard to any proposition implying the existence of a material thing, that we are not somehow being deceived; but at the same time one may object to this statement on the ground that it is misleading. It is misleading because it suggests that the state of 'being sure' is one the attainment of which is conceivable, but unfortunately not within our power. *But,* in fact, *the conception of such a state is self-contradictory.* For in order to be sure, in this sense, that we were not being deceived, we should have to have completed an infinite series of verifications; and it is an analytic proposition that one cannot run through all the members of an infinite series. . . . Accordingly, what we should say, if we wish to avoid misunderstanding, is not that we can never be certain that any of the propositions in which we express our perceptual judgments are true, but rather that *the notion of certainty does not apply to propositions of this kind.* It applies to the a priori propositions of logic and mathematics, and the fact that it does apply to them is an essential mark of distinction between them and empirical propositions.[9]

The reason, then, that Ayer is so confident that it never has been and never will be right for anyone to say of a material-thing statement that he knows it for certain, is that he thinks it is self-contradictory to say that a material-thing statement is known for certain. He thinks that the phrase "known for certain" is properly applied only to a priori statements, and not to empirical statements. The philosophical statement "We do not know for certain the truth of any material-thing statement" is a misleading way of expressing the proposition "The phrase 'known for certain' is not properly applied to material-thing statements." Now Moore's reply, "Both of us know for certain that there are several chairs in this room, and how absurd it would be to suggest that we do not know it, but only believe it, or that it is highly probable but not really certain!" is a misleading way of saying "It is a proper way of speaking to say that we know for certain that there are several chairs in this room, and it would be an improper way of speaking to say that we only

---

[9] Ayer, *The Foundations of Empirical Knowledge, op. cit.,* pp. 44f. My italics.

believe it, or that it is only highly probable!" Both the philosophical statement and Moore's reply to it are disguised linguistic statements.

In this as in all the other cases Moore is right. What his reply does is to give us a *paradigm* of absolute certainty, just as in the case previously discussed his reply gave us a paradigm of seeing something not a part of one's brain. What his reply does is to appeal to our language-sense; to make us feel how queer and wrong it would be to say, when we sat in a room seeing and touching chairs, that we *believed* there were chairs but did not know it for certain, or that it was only highly probable that there were chairs. Just as in the previous case his reply made us feel how perfectly proper it is in certain cases to say that one sees a desk or a pen, and how grossly improper it would be in such cases to say that one sees a part of one's brain. Moore's reply reminds us of the fact that if a child who was learning the language were to say, in a situation where we were sitting in a room with chairs about, that it was "highly probable" that there were chairs there, we should smile, *and correct his language*. It reminds us of such facts as this: that if we were driving at a rapid speed past some plants in a cultivated field, it might be proper to say "It's highly probable that they are tomato plants, although we can't tell for certain"; but if we had ourselves planted the seeds, hoed and watered them, and watched them grow, and finally gathered the ripe tomatoes off them, then to say the same thing would, to use John Wisdom's phrase, "raise a titter." By reminding us of how we ordinarily use the expressions "know for certain" and "highly probable," Moore's reply constitutes a refutation of the philosophical statement that we can never have certain knowledge of material-thing statements. It reminds us that there *is* an ordinary use of the phrase "know for certain" in which it is applied to empirical statements; and so shows us that Ayer is wrong when he says that "The notion of certainty does not apply to propositions of this kind."

Indeed the notion of *logical* certainty does not apply to empirical statements. The mark of a logically certain proposition, i.e., an a priori proposition, is that the negative of it is self-contradictory. Any proposition which has this character we do not *call* an empirical statement. One of the main sources of the philosophical statement, "We can't ever know for certain the truth of any empirical statement," has been the desire to point out that empirical statements do not have logical certainty. But this truism has been expressed in a false way. The truth is not that the phrase "I know for certain" has no proper application to empirical statements, but that the sense which it has in its application to empirical statements is *different* from the sense which it has in its application to a priori statements. Moore's refutation consists simply in pointing out that it has *an* application to empirical statements.

II

It may be objected: "Ordinary men are ignorant, misinformed, and therefore frequently mistaken. Ordinary language is the language of ordinary men. You talk as if the fact that a certain phrase is used in ordinary language implies that, when people use that phrase, what they say is *true*. You talk as if the fact that people *say* 'I know for certain that p,' where p is a material-thing statement, implies that they *do* know for certain. But this is ridiculous! At one time everyone said that the earth was flat, when it was actually round. Everyone was mistaken; and there is no reason why in these philosophical cases the philosophers should not be right and everyone else wrong."

In order to answer this objection, we need to consider that there are two ways in which a person may be wrong when he makes an empirical statement. First, he may be making a mistake as to what the empirical facts are. Second, he may know all right what the empirical facts are, but may use the wrong language to describe those facts. We might call the first "being mistaken about the facts," and the second "using incorrect language" or "using improper language" or "using wrong language."

It is true that at one time everyone said that the earth was flat, and what everyone said was wrong. Everyone believed that if you got into a ship and sailed west you would finally come to the edge and fall off. They did not believe that if you kept on sailing west you would come back to where you started from. When they said that the earth was flat, they were wrong. The way in which their statement was wrong was that they were making a mistake about the facts, not that they were using incorrect language. They were using perfectly correct language to describe what they thought to be the case. In the sense in which they said what was wrong, it is perfectly possible for *everyone* to say what is wrong.

Now suppose a case where two people agree as to what the empirical facts are, and yet disagree in their statements. For example, two people are looking at an animal; they have a clear, close-up view of it. Their descriptions of the animal are in perfect agreement. Yet one of them says it is a fox, the other says it is a wolf. Their disagreement could be called linguistic. There is, of course, a right and a wrong with respect to linguistic disagreements. One or the other, or both of them, is using incorrect language.

Now suppose that there were a case like the one preceding with this exception: that the one who says it is a wolf, not only agrees with the other man as to what the characteristics of the animal are, but further-more *agrees that that sort of animal is ordinarily called a fox*. If he were to continue to insist that it is a wolf, we can see how absurd would be his position. He would be saying that, although the other man was using an expression to describe a certain situation which was the expression ordinarily employed to describe that sort of situation, nevertheless the other man was using incorrect language. What makes his statement absurd is that ordinary language *is* correct language.

The authors of the philosophical paradoxes commit this very absurdity, though in a subtle and disguised way. When the philosopher says that we never really perceive material things, since all that we really perceive are sense-data and sense-data are not material things nor parts of material things, he does not disagree with the ordinary man about any question of empirical fact. Compare his case with the case of two men who are proceeding along a road. One of them says that he sees trees in the distance; the other says that it is not true that he sees trees—that it is really a mirage he sees. Now this is a genuine dispute as to what the facts are, and this dispute could be settled by their going further along the road, to the place where the trees are thought to be.

But the philosopher who says that the ordinary person is mistaken when he says that he sees the cat in a tree does not mean that he sees a squirrel rather than a cat; does not mean that it is a mirage; does not mean that it is an hallucination. He will agree that the facts of the situation are what we should ordinarily describe by the expression "seeing a cat in a tree." Nevertheless, he says that the man does not *really* see a cat; he sees only some sense-data of a cat. Now if it gives the philosopher pleasure always to substitute the expression "I see some sense-data of my wife" for the expression "I see my wife," etc., then he is at liberty thus to express himself, *providing* he warns people beforehand so that they will understand him. But when he says that the man does not *really* see a cat, he commits a great absurdity; for he implies that a person can use an expression to describe a certain state of affairs, which is the expression ordinarily used to describe just such a state of affairs, and yet be using incorrect language.

One thing which has led philosophers to attack ordinary language has been their supposing that certain expressions of ordinary language are self-contradictory.[10] Some philosophers have thought that any assertion of the existence of a material thing, e.g., "There's a chair in the corner," is self-contradictory. Some have thought that any assertion of the perception of a material thing, e.g., "I see a fly on the ceiling," is self-contradictory. Some have thought that any assertion of the existence of an unperceived material thing, e.g., "The house burned down, when no

---

[10] I think that this is really behind *all* attacks upon ordinary language. For how could a philosopher hold, on nonempirical grounds, that the using of a certain expression will *always* produce a false statement, unless he held that the expression is self-contradictory?

one was around," is self-contradictory. Some have seemed to think that statements describing spatial relations, e.g., "The stove is to the left of the icebox," are self-contradictory.

Some have seemed to think that statements describing temporal relations, e.g., "Charles came later than the others, but before the doors were closed," are self-contradictory. Some philosophers think that it is self-contradictory to assert that an empirical statement is known for certain, e.g., "I know for certain that the tank is half-full."

The assumption underlying all of these theories is that an ordinary expression *can* be self-contradictory. This assumption seems to me to be false. By an "ordinary expression" I mean an expression which has an ordinary use, i.e., which is ordinarily used to describe a certain sort of situation. By this I do not mean that the expression need be one which is frequently used. It need only be an expression which *would* be used to describe situations of a certain sort, if situations of that sort were to exist, or were believed to exist. To be an ordinary expression it must have a commonly accepted *use*; it need not be the case that it is ever *used*. All of the above statements, which various philosophers have thought were self-contradictory, are ordinary expressions in this sense.

The reason that no ordinary expression is self-contradictory is that a self-contradictory expression is an expression which would *never* be used to describe *any* sort of situation. It does not have a descriptive usage. An ordinary expression is an expression which would be used to describe a certain sort of situation; and since it would be used to describe a certain sort of situation, it *does* describe that sort of situation. A self-contradictory expression, on the contrary, describes nothing. It is possible, of course, to *construct* out of ordinary expressions an expression which is self-contradictory. But the expression so constructed is not itself an ordinary expression—i.e., not an expression which has a descriptive use.

The proposition that no ordinary expression is self-contradictory is a tautology, but perhaps an illuminating one. We do not *call* an expression which has a descriptive use a self-contradictory expression. For example, the expression "It is and it isn't" looks like a self-contradictory expression. But it has a descriptive use. If, for example, a very light mist is falling—so light that it would not be quite correct to say that it was *raining,* yet heavy enough to make it not quite correct to say that it was *not* raining—and someone, asking for information, asked whether it was raining, we might reply "Well, it is and it isn't." We should not say that the phrase, used in this connection, is self-contradictory.

The point is that, even if an expression has the appearance of being self-contradictory, we do not *call* it self-contradictory, providing it has a use. Nor do we say of *any* expression which is used to describe or refer to a certain state of affairs that *in that use* it is self-contradictory. It follows that no ordinary expression is, in any ordinary use of that expression, self-contradictory. Whenever a philosopher claims that an ordinary expression is self-contradictory, he has misinterpreted the meaning of that ordinary expression.

A philosophical paradox asserts that, whenever a person uses a certain expression, what he says is false. This could be either because the sort of situation described by the expression never does, *in fact,* occur; or because the expression is self-contradictory. Now the point of replying to the philosophical statement, by showing that the expression in question does have a descriptive use in ordinary language, is to prove, first, that the expression is not self-contradictory; and, second, that therefore the only ground for maintaining that when people use the expression what they say is always false will have to be the claim that *on the basis of empirical evidence* it is known that the sort of situation described by the expression never has occurred and never will occur. But it is abundantly clear that the philosopher offers no empirical evidence for his paradox.

The objection set down at the beginning of this section contains the claim that it does not follow from the fact that a certain expression is used in ordinary language that, on any occasion when people use that expression, what they say is true. It does not follow for example, from the fact that the expression "to the left of" is an ordinary expression, that anything ever *is* to the left of another thing. It does not follow from the fact that the expression "it is certain that" is an ordinary expression applied to empirical statements that any empirical statements ever *are* certain. Let us, next, consider this question.

The expression "There's a ghost" has a descriptive use. It is, in my sense of the phrase, an ordinary expression; and it does not follow from the fact that it is an ordinary expression that there ever have been any ghosts. But it is important to note that people can learn the meaning of the word "ghost" without actually seeing any ghosts. That is, the meaning of the word "ghost" can be explained to them in terms of the meanings of words which they already know. It seems to me that there is an enormous difference in this respect between the learning of the word "ghost" and the learning of expressions like "earlier," "later," "to the left of," "behind," "above," "material things," "it is possible that," "it is certain that." The difference is that, whereas you can teach a person the meaning of the word "ghost" without showing him an instance of the true application of that word, you cannot teach a person the meaning of these other expressions without showing him instances of the true application of those expressions. People could not have learned the meaning of the expressions "to the left of," or "above," unless they had actually been shown instances of one thing being to the left of another, and one thing being above another. In short, they could not have learned the meanings of expressions which describe spatial relations without having been acquainted with some instances of spatial relations. Likewise, people could not have learned the use of expressions describing temporal relations, like "earlier" and "later," unless they had been shown examples of things standing in these temporal relations. Nor could people have learned the difference between "seeing a material thing" and "seeing an after-image" or "having an hallucination" unless they had actually been acquainted with cases of seeing a material thing. And people could not have learned the meaning of "it is probable that," as applied to empirical statements, and of "it is certain that," as applied to empirical statements, unless they had been shown cases of empirical probability and cases of empirical certainty, and had seen the difference or differences between them.

In the case of all expressions the meanings of which must be *shown* and cannot be explained, as can the meaning of "ghost," it follows, from the fact that they are ordinary expressions in the language, that there have been *many* situations of the kind which they describe; otherwise so many people could not have learned the correct use of those expressions. Whenever a philosophical paradox asserts, therefore, with regard to such an expression, that always when that expression is used the use of it produces a false statement, then to prove that the expression is an *ordinary* expression is completely to refute the paradox.

III

An empirical statement can be paradoxical and not be false. A philosophical statement cannot be paradoxical and not be false. This is because they are paradoxical in totally different ways. If an empirical statement is paradoxical, that is because it asserts the existence of empirical facts which everyone or almost everyone believed to be incompatible with the existence of other well-established empirical facts. But if a philosophical statement is paradoxical, that is because it asserts the impropriety of an ordinary form of speech. It is possible for everyone to be mistaken about certain matters of empirical fact. That is why an empirical statement can be paradoxical and yet true. But it is not possible for an ordinary form of speech to be improper. That is to say, ordinary language is correct language.

When a philosopher says, for example, that all empirical statements are hypotheses,[11] or that a priori statements are really rules of grammar,[12] Moore at once attacks. He attacks because he is sensitive to the

---

[11] "Empirical statements are one and all hypotheses. . . ." Ayer, *Language, Truth, and Logic, op. cit.*, p. 132.

[12] I do not know that *exactly* this statement has ever been made in print, but it has been made in discussions in Cambridge, England.

violations of ordinary language which are implicit in such statements. " '49 minus 22 equals 27' a *rule of grammar?* 'Napoleon was defeated at Waterloo' an *hypothesis?* What an absurd way of talking!" Moore's attacks bring home to us that our ordinary use of the expressions "rule of grammar" and "hypothesis" is very different from that suggested by the philosophical statements. If a child learning the language were to call "49 minus 22 equals 27" a *rule of grammar,* or "Napoleon was defeated at Waterloo" an *hypothesis,* we should *correct* him. We should say that such language is not a proper way of speaking.

The reason that the philosopher makes his paradoxical statement that all empirical propositions are hypotheses is that he is impressed by and wishes to emphasize a certain similarity between the empirical statements which we should ordinarily call hypotheses and the empirical statements which we should ordinarily call, not hypotheses, but absolutely certain truths. The similarity between the empirical proposition the truth of which we say is not perfectly established, but which we will assume in order to use it as a working hypothesis, and the empirical proposition the truth of which we say is absolutely certain, is that neither of them possesses *logical* certainty. That is, neither of them has a self-contradictory negative. The falsehood of the absolutely certain empirical proposition, as well as of the hypothesis, is a logical possibility. The philosopher, wishing to emphasize this similarity, does so by saying that all empirical statements are really hypotheses. Likewise, one of the main sources of the paradoxical statement that no empirical statements ever have absolute certainty but at most high probability lies, as we have said, in the desire to stress this same similarity. This linguistic device of speaking paradoxically, which the philosopher adopts in order to stress a similarity, does of course ignore the *dis*similarities. It ignores the dissimilarities, which *justify* the distinction made in ordinary language, between absolutely certain empirical propositions and empirical propositions which are only hypotheses or have only high probability.

Let us consider another example of the philosophical procedure of employing a paradox in order to emphasize a similarity or a difference. Philosophers have sometimes made the statement "All words are vague." It is the desire to emphasize a similarity between words with vague meanings and words with clear meanings which has tempted the philosophers to utter this paradox. The meaning of a word is vague, if it is the case that in a large number of situations where the question is raised as to whether the word applies or not, people who know the use of the word and who know all the facts of the situations are undecided as to whether the word does apply or not, or disagree among themselves without being able to come to any consensus of opinion. Let us call such situations "undecidable cases." A word is vague, then, if with regard to the question of its application there is a *large* number of undecidable cases.

But even with respect to the words which we should ordinarily say have clear meanings, it is possible to produce undecidable cases. The only difference between the clear words and the vague ones is that with respect to the former the number of undecidable cases is relatively smaller. But then, says the philosopher, the difference between a large number of undecidable cases and a small number is only a difference of *degree*! He is, therefore, tempted to say that *all* words are really vague. But, we might ask, why should not the use of the words "vague" and "clear," in ordinary language, simply serve to call attention to those differences of degree?

Similarly, a philosophizing biologist, finding it impossible to draw a sharp line separating the characteristics of inanimate things from the characteristics of animate things, may be tempted to proclaim that all matter is really animate. What he says is philosophical, paradoxical, and false. For it constitutes an offense against ordinary language, in the learning of which we learn to call things like fish and fowl animate, and things like rocks and tables inanimate.

Certain words of our language operate in pairs, e.g., "large" and "small," "animate" and "inanimate," "vague" and "clear," "certain" and "probable." In their use in ordinary language a member of a pair *requires* its opposite—for animate is *contrasted* with inanimate, probability with certainty, vagueness with clearness. Now there are certain features about the criteria for the use of the words in these pairs which tempt philosophers to wish to remove from use one member of the pair. When the philosopher says that all words are really vague, he is proposing that we never apply the word "clear" anymore, i.e., proposing that we abolish its use.

But suppose that we did *change* our language in such a way that we made the philosophical statements true—that is, made it true that it was no longer correct to call any material thing inanimate, no longer correct to call any empirical statement certain, no longer correct to say of any word that its meaning is clear. Would this be an improvement?

It is important to see that by such a move we should have gained nothing whatever. The word in our revised language would have to do double duty. The word "vague" would have to perform the function previously performed by two words, "vague" and "clear." But it could not perform this function. For it was essential to the meaning of the word "vague," in its previous use, that vagueness was *contrasted* with clearness. In the revised language vagueness could be contrasted with nothing. The word "vague" would simply be dropped as a useless word. And we should be compelled to adopt into the revised language a new pair of words with which to express the same distinctions formerly expressed by the words "clear" and "vague." The revision of our language would have accomplished nothing.

The paradoxical statements of the philosophers are produced, we have suggested, by their desire to emphasize similarities or differences between the criteria for the use of certain words. For example, the statement that no empirical propositions are certain arises from the desire to stress the similarity between the criteria for applying the phrases "absolutely certain" and "highly probable" to empirical propositions; and also from the desire to stress the difference between the criteria for applying "certain" to empirical statements, and for applying it to a priori statements. The desire to stress various similarities and differences tempts the philosophers to make their paradoxes.

The reason I have talked so much about the nature of paradoxical philosophical statements and the temptations which produce them is to throw light on Moore's role as a philosopher. A striking thing about Moore is that he never succumbs to such temptations. On the contrary, he takes his stand upon ordinary language and defends it against every attack, against every paradox. The philosophizing of most of the more important philosophers has consisted in their more or less subtly repudiating ordinary language. Moore's philosophizing has consisted mostly in his refuting the repudiators of ordinary language.

The role which Moore, the Great Refuter, has played in the history of philosophy has been mainly a destructive one. (His most important constructive theory, the theory that good is a simple indefinable quality like yellow, was itself a natural outcome of his own destructive treatment of innumerable attempts to define "good.") To realize how much of philosophy consists of attacks on ordinary language, on common sense, and to see that ordinary language must be right, is to see the importance and the justification of Moore's destructive function in philosophy.

It might be asked: "You say that the philosopher's paradox arises from his desire to stress a similarity or a difference in the criteria for the use of certain expressions. But if the similarity or the difference does really exist, and if all that his philosophical statement does is to call attention to it, why not let him have his paradox? What harm is there in it?" The answer is that if that were the whole of the matter, then there would be no harm in it. But what invariably happens is that the philosopher is misled by the form of his philosophical statement into imagining that it is an empirical statement. "There is no certainty about empirical matters" is so very much like "There is no certainty about the future of the present generation." "What one really sees when one looks at a thing is a part of one's brain" is so very like "What really happens when one sees a thing is that light rays from it strike the retina." Misled by the similarity in appearance of these two sorts of statements, and knowing that the paradoxicalness of empirical statements is no objection to their being true, the philosopher imagines that his paradox is really true—that common sense is really wrong in supposing that empirical matters are ever certain, that any words ever have clear meanings, that anything other than a part of one's brain is ever seen, that anything ever does happen later or earlier than something else, and so on.

When the philosopher supposes that his paradox is literally true, it is salutary to refute him. The fact that the authors of the paradoxes nearly always fancy themselves to be right and common sense to be wrong, and that they then need to have it proved to them that their statements are false, explains Moore's great importance in philosophy. No one can rival Moore as a refuter because no one has so keen a nose for paradoxes. Moore's extraordinarily powerful language-sense enables him to detect the most subtle violations of ordinary language.

Two things may be said against Moore's method of refutation.[13] In the first place, it often fails to convince the author of the paradox that he is wrong. If, for example, the paradox is that no one ever knows for certain that any other person is having sensations, feelings, experiences, and Moore replies "On the contrary, I know that you now see and hear me," it is likely that the man who made the paradox will not feel refuted. This is largely because Moore's reply fails to bring out the linguistic, nonempirical nature of the paradox. It sounds as if he were opposing one empirical proposition with another, contradictory, empirical proposition. His reply does not make it clear that what the paradox does is to attack an ordinary form of speech as an incorrect form of speech, *without disagreeing as to what the empirical facts are,* on *any* occasion on which that ordinary form of speech is used.

In the second place, Moore's style of refutation does not get at the sources of the philosophical troubles which produce the paradoxes. Even if it shows the philosopher that his paradox is false, it only leaves him dissatisfied. It does not explain to him what it was that made him want to attack ordinary language. And it does not remove the temptation to attack ordinary language by showing how fruitless that attack is. In short, even if Moore does succeed in making the philosopher feel refuted, he does not succeed in curing the philosophical puzzlement which caused the philosopher to make the paradox which needs to be refuted.

Although Moore's philosophical method is an incomplete method, it is the essential first step in a complete method. The way to treat a philosophical paradox is first of all to resist it, to prove it false. Because, if the philosopher is pleased with his paradox, fancies it to be true, then you can do nothing with him. It is only when he is dissatisfied with his paradox, feels refuted, that it is possible to clear up for him the philosophical problem of which his paradox is a manifestation.

However, to say that Moore's technique of refutation is the essential first step in the complete philosophical method does not adequately de-

---

[13] This must be taken as qualifying my previous statement that Moore's refutations are *good* ones.

scribe the importance of the part he has played in the history of philosophy. Moore's great historical role consists in the fact that he has been perhaps the first philosopher to sense that any philosophical statement which violates ordinary language is false, and consistently to defend ordinary language against its philosophical violators.[14]

---

[14] My present belief (1963) is that my article gives an accurate description of Moore's reaction to typical philosophical assertions, and also that in most fundamental points the article is sound. I do not like its youthfully overconfident tone, my remarks about "paradoxical" philosophical statements are unnecessarily paradoxical, what I say about *certainty* is certainly unsatisfactory, and I no longer think that Moore is to be understood as presenting *paradigms* of perception, knowledge, and so on. For a somewhat different interpretation of Moore's defense of ordinary language the reader is referred to the lecture "George Edward Moore" in my book *Knowledge and Certainty* (Englewood Cliffs, N.J.: Prentice-Hall, Inc., 1963). [Note added in this edition.]

ORDINARY LANGUAGE

GILBERT RYLE

Philosophers' arguments have frequently turned on references to what we do and do not say or, more strongly, on what we can and cannot say. Such arguments are present in the writings of Plato and are common in those of Aristotle.

In recent years, some philosophers, having become feverishly exercised about the nature and methodology of their calling, have made much of arguments of this kind. Other philosophers have repudiated them. Their disputes on the merits of these arguments have not been edifying, since both sides have been apt to garble the question. I want to ungarble it.

"ORDINARY"

There is one phrase which recurs in this dispute, the phrase "the use of ordinary language." It is often, quite erroneously, taken to be para-

From The Philosophical Review, *Vol. LXII* (1953). *Reprinted by permission of the author and* The Philosophical Review.

phrased by "ordinary linguistic usage." Some of the partisans assert that all philosophical questions are questions about the use of ordinary language, or that all philosophical questions are solved or are about to be solved by considering ordinary linguistic usage.

Postponing the examination of the notion of *linguistic usage,* I want to begin by contrasting the phrase "the use of ordinary language" with the similar-seeming but totally different phrase "the ordinary use of the expression '. . . .'" When people speak of the use of ordinary language, the word "ordinary" is in implicit or explicit contrast with "out-of-the-way," "esoteric," "technical," "poetical," "notational" or, sometimes, "archaic." "Ordinary" means "common," "current," "colloquial," "vernacular," "natural," "prosaic," "nonnotational," "on the tongue of Everyman," and is usually in contrast with dictions which only a few people know how to use, such as the technical terms or artificial symbolisms of lawyers, theologians, economists, philosophers, cartographers, mathematicians, symbolic logicians and players of Royal Tennis. There is no sharp boundary between "common" and "uncommon," "technical" and "untechnical" or "old-fashioned" and "current." Is "carburetor" a word in common use or only in rather uncommon use? Is "purl" on the lips of Everyman, or on the lips only of Everywoman? What of "manslaughter," "inflation," "quotient" and "off-side"? On the other hand, no one would hesitate on which side of this no-man's-land to locate "isotope" or "bread," "material implication" or "if," "transfinite cardinal" or "eleven," "ween" or "suppose." The edges of "ordinary" are blurred, but usually we are in no doubt whether a diction does or does not belong to ordinary parlance.

But in the other phrase, "the ordinary use of the expression '. . . ,'" "ordinary" is not in contrast with "esoteric," "archaic" or "specialist," etc. It is in contrast with "nonstock" or "nonstandard." We can contrast the stock or standard use of a fish-knife or sphygmomanometer with some nonregulation use of it. The stock use of a fish-knife is to cut up fish with; but it might be used for cutting seed potatoes or as a heliograph. A sphygmomanometer might, for all I know, be used for checking tire pressures; but this is not its standard use. Whether an implement or instrument is a common or a specialist one, there remains the distinction between its stock use and nonstock uses of it. If a term is a highly technical term, or a nontechnical term, there remains the distinction between its stock use and nonstock uses of it. If a term is a highly technical term, most people will not know its stock use or, a fortiori, any nonstock uses of it either, if it has any. If it is a vernacular term, then nearly everyone will know its stock use, and most people will also know some nonstock uses of it, if it has any. There are lots of words, like "of," "have" and "object," which have no one stock use, any more than string, paper, brass and pocketknives have just one stock use.

Lots of words have not got any nonstock uses. "Sixteen" has, I think, none; nor has "daffodil." Nor, maybe, have collar-studs. Nonstock uses of a word are, e.g., metaphorical, hyperbolical, poetical, stretched and deliberately restricted uses of it. Besides contrasting the stock use with certain nonstock uses, we often want to contrast the stock use of an expression with certain alleged, suggested, or recommended uses of it. This is a contrast not between the regular use and irregular uses, but between the regular use and what the regular use is alleged to be or what it is recommended that it should be.

When we speak of the ordinary or stock use of a word we need not be characterizing it in any further way, e.g., applauding or recommending it or giving it any testimonial. We need not be appealing to or basing anything on its stock-ness. The words "ordinary," "standard" and "stock" can serve merely to refer to a use, without describing it. They are philosophically colorless and can be easily dispensed with. When we speak of the regular night-watchman, we are merely indicating the night-watchman whom we know independently to be the one usually on the job; we are not yet giving any information about him or paying any tribute to his regularity. When we speak of the standard spelling of a word or the standard gauge of British railway tracks, we are not describing or recommending or countenancing this spelling or this gauge; we are giving a reference to it which we expect our hearers to get without hesitation. Sometimes, naturally, this indication does not work. Sometimes the stock use in one place is different from its stock use in another, as with "suspenders." Sometimes, its stock use at one period differs from its stock use at another, as with "nice." A dispute about which of two or five uses is the stock use is not a philosophical dispute about any one of those uses. It is therefore philosophically uninteresting, though settlement of it is sometimes requisite for communication between philosophers.

If I want to talk about a nonstock use of a word or fish-knife, it is not enough to try to refer to it by the phrase "the nonstock use of it," for there may be any number of such nonstock uses. To call my hearer's attention to a particular nonstock use of it, I have to give some description of it, for example, to cite a special context in which the word is known to be used in a nonstock way.

This, though always possible, is not often necessary for the stock use of an expression, although in philosophical debates one is sometimes required to do it, since one's fellow-philosophers are at such pains to pretend that they cannot think what its stock use is—a difficulty which, of course, they forget all about when they are teaching children or foreigners how to use it, and when they are consulting dictionaries.

It is easy now to see that learning or teaching the ordinary or stock use of an expression need not be, though it may be, learning or teaching the use of an ordinary or vernacular expression, just as learning or teaching the standard use of an instrument need not be, though it can be, learning or teaching the use of a household utensil. Most words and instruments, whether out-of-the-way or common, have their stock uses and may or may not also have nonstock uses as well.

A philosopher who maintained that certain philosophical questions are questions about the ordinary or stock uses of certain expressions would not therefore be committing himself to the view that they are questions about the uses of ordinary or colloquial expressions. He could admit that the noun "infinitesimals" is not on the lips of Everyman and still maintain that Berkeley was examining the ordinary or stock use of "infinitesimals," namely the standard way, if not the only way, in which this word was employed by mathematical specialists. Berkeley was not examining the use of a colloquial word; he was examining the regular or standard use of a relatively esoteric word. We are not contradicting ourselves if we say that he was examining the ordinary use of an unordinary expression.

Clearly a lot of philosophical discussions are of this type. In the philosophy of law, biology, physics, mathematics, formal logic, theology, psychology and grammar, technical concepts have to be examined, and these concepts are what are expressed by more or less recherché dictions. Doubtless this examination embodies attempts to elucidate in untechnical terms the technical terms of this or that specialist theory, but this very attempt involves discussing the ordinary or stock uses of these technical terms.

Doubtless, too, study by philosophers of the stock uses of expressions which we all employ has a certain primacy over their study of the stock uses of expressions which only, e.g., scientific or legal specialists employ. These specialists explain to novices the stock uses of their terms of art partly by talking to them in nonesoteric terms; they do not also have to explain to them the stock uses of these nonesoteric terms. Untechnical terminology is, in this way, basic to technical terminologies. Hard cash has this sort of primacy over checks and bills of exchange—as well as the same inconveniences when large and complex transactions are afoot.

Doubtless, finally, some of the cardinal problems of philosophy are set by the existence of logical tangles not in this as opposed to that branch of specialist theory, but in the thought and the discourse of everyone, specialists and nonspecialists alike. The concepts of *cause, evidence, knowledge, mistake, ought, can,* etc., are not the perquisites of any particular groups of people. We employ them before we begin to develop or follow specialist theories; and we could not follow or develop such theories unless we could already employ these concepts. They belong to the rudiments of all thinking, including specialist thinking. But it does not follow from this that all philosophical questions are questions about such rudimentary concepts. The architect must indeed be careful about the materials of his building; but it is not only about these that he must be careful.

"USE"

But now for a further point. The phrase "the ordinary (i.e., stock) use of the expression '. . .' " is often so spoken that the stress is made to fall on the word "expression" or else on the word "ordinary" and the word "use" is slurred over. The reverse ought to be the case. The operative word is *"use."*

Hume's question was not about the word "cause"; it was about the *use* of "cause." It was just as much about the *use* of "Ursache." For the use of "cause" is the same as the use of "Ursache," though "cause" is not the same word as "Ursache." Hume's question was not a question about a bit of the English language in any way in which it was not a question about a bit of the German language. The job done with the English word "cause" is not an English job, or a continental job. What I do with my Nottingham-made boots—namely walk in them—is not Nottingham-made; but nor is it Leicester-made or Derby-made. The transactions I perform with a sixpenny-bit have neither milled nor un-milled edges; they have no edges at all. We might discuss what I can and cannot do with a sixpenny-bit, namely what I can and cannot buy with it, what change I should and should not give or take for it, and so on; but such a discussion would not be a discussion about the date, ingredients, shape, color or provenance of the coin. It is a discussion about the purchasing power of this coin, or of any other coin of the same value, and not about *this coin*. It is not a numismatic discussion, but a commercial or financial discussion. Putting the stress on the word "use" helps to bring out the important fact that the inquiry is an inquiry not into the other features or properties of the word or coin or pair of boots, but only into what is done with it, or with anything else with which we do the same thing. That is why it is so misleading to classify philo-sophical questions as linguistic questions—or as nonlinguistic questions.

It is, I think, only in fairly recent years that philosophers have picked up the trick of talking about the use of expressions, and even made a virtue of so talking. Our forefathers, at one time, talked instead of the *concepts* or *ideas* corresponding to expressions. This was in many ways a very convenient idiom, and one which in most situations we do well to retain. It had the drawback, though, that it encouraged people to start Platonic or Lockean hares about the status and provenance of these concepts or ideas. The impression was given that a philosopher who wanted to discuss, say, the concept of *cause* or *infinitesimal* or *remorse* was under some obligation to start by deciding whether concepts have a supramundane, or only a psychological existence; whether they are transcendent intuitables or only private introspectibles.

Later on, when philosophers were in revolt against psychologism in logic, there was a vogue for another idiom, the idiom of talking about the *meanings* of expressions, and the phrase "the concept of cause" was replaced by the phrase "the meaning of the word 'cause' or of any other with the same meaning." This new idiom was also subject to anti-Platonic and anti-Lockean cavils; but its biggest drawback was a different one. Philosophers and logicians were at that time the victims of a special and erroneous theory about meaning. They construed the verb "to mean" as standing for a relation between an expression and some other entity. The meaning of an expression was taken to be an entity which had that expression for its name. So studying the meaning of the phrase "the solar system" was supposed or half-supposed to be the same thing as studying the solar system. It was partly in reaction against this erroneous view that philosophers came to prefer the idiom "the use of the expressions '. . . caused . . .' and '. . . the solar system.'" We are accustomed to talking of the use of safety pins, banisters, tableknives, badges and gestures; and this familiar idiom neither connotes nor seems to connote any queer relations to any queer entities. It draws our attention to the teachable procedures and techniques of handling or employing things, without suggesting unwanted correlates. Learning how to manage a canoe-paddle, a traveler's check or a postage stamp is not being introduced to an extra entity. Nor is learning how to manage the words "if," "ought" and "limit."

There is another merit in this idiom. Where we can speak of managing, handling and employing we can speak of mismanaging, mishandling and misemploying. There are rules to keep or break, codes to observe or flout. Learning to use expressions, like learning to use coins, stamps, checks and hockey-sticks, involves learning to do certain things with them and not others; when to do certain things with them, and when not to do them. Among the things that we learn in the process of learning to use linguistic expressions are what we may vaguely call "rules of logic"; for example, that though Mother and Father can both be tall, they cannot both be taller than one another; or that though uncles can be rich or poor, fat or thin, they cannot be male or female, but only male. Where it would sound implausible to say that concepts or ideas or meanings might be meaningless or absurd, there is no such implausibility in asserting that someone might use a certain expression absurdly. An attempted or suggested way of operating with an expres-

sion may be logically illegitimate or impossible, but a universal or a
state of consciousness or a meaning cannot be logically legitimate or
illegitimate.

"USE" AND "UTILITY"

On the other hand there are inconveniences in talking much of the
uses of expressions. People are liable to construe "use" in one of the
ways which English certainly does permit, namely as a synonym of
"utility" or "usefulness." They then suppose that to discuss the use of
an expression is to discuss what it is useful for or how useful it is. Sometimes such considerations are philosophically profitable. But it is easy
to see that discussing the use (versus uselessness) of something is quite
different from discussing the use (versus misuse) of it, i.e., the way,
method or manner of using it. The female driver may learn what is the
utility of a spark plug, but learning this is not learning how to operate
with a spark plug. She does not have or lack skills or competences with
spark plugs, as she does with steering wheels, coins, words and knives.
Her spark plugs manage themselves; or, rather, they are not managed at
all. They just function automatically, until they cease to function. They
are useful, even indispensable to her. But she does not manage or mismanage them.

Conversely, a person who has learned how to whistle tunes may not
find the whistling of tunes at all useful or even pleasant to others or to
himself. He manages, or sometimes mismanages his lips, tongue and
breath; and, more indirectly, manages or mismanages the notes he produces. He has got the trick of it; he can show us and perhaps even tell
us how the trick is performed. But it is a useless trick. The question
"How do you use your breath or your lips in whistling?" has a positive
and complicated answer. The question "What is the use, or utility, of
whistling?" has a negative and simple one. The former is a request for
the details of a technique; the latter is not. Questions about the use of an
expression are often, though not always, questions about the way to
operate with it; not questions about what the employer of it needs it for.
They are How-questions, not What-for-questions. This latter sort of
question can be asked, but it is seldom necessary to ask it, since the
answer is usually obvious. In a foreign country, I do not ask what a
centime or a peseta is for; what I do ask is how many of them I have
to give for a certain article, or how many of them I am to expect to get
in exchange for a half-crown. I want to know what its purchasing power
is; not that it is for making purchases with.

"USE" AND "USAGE"

Much more insidious than this confusion between the way of operating with something and its usefulness is the confusion between a "use,"
i.e., a way of operating with something, and a "usage." Lots of philosophers, whose dominant good resolution is to discern logico-linguistic differences, talk without qualms as if "use" and "usage" were synonyms.
This is just a howler; for which there is little excuse except that in the
archaic phrase "use and wont," "use" could, perhaps, be replaced by
"usage"; that "used to" does mean "accustomed to"; and that to be
hardly used is to suffer hard usage.

A usage is a custom, practice, fashion or vogue. It can be local or
widespread, obsolete or current, rural or urban, vulgar or academic.
There cannot be a misusage any more than there can be a miscustom or a
misvogue. The methods of discovering linguistic usages are the methods
of philologists.

By contrast, a way of operating with a razor-blade, a word, a traveler's check, or a canoe-paddle is a technique, knack, or method. Learning it is learning how to do the thing; it is not finding out sociological
generalities, not even sociological generalities about other people who do
similar or different things with razor-blades, words, travelers' checks, or
canoe-paddles. Robinson Crusoe might find out for himself how to make
and how to throw boomerangs; but this discovery would tell him nothing about those Australian aborigines who do in fact make and use them
in the same way. The description of a conjuring-trick is not the description of all the conjurors who perform or have performed that trick. On
the contrary, in order to describe the possessors of the trick, we should
have already to be able to give some sort of description of the trick itself.
Mrs. Beeton tells us how to make omelets; but she gives us no information about Parisian chefs. Baedeker might tell us about Parisian chefs,
and tell us which of them make omelets; but if he wanted to tell us how
they make omelets, he would have to describe their techniques in the
way that Mrs. Beeton describes the technique of making omelets. Descriptions of usages presuppose descriptions of uses, i.e., ways or techniques of doing the thing, the more or less widely prevailing practice of
doing which constitutes the usage.

There is an important difference between the employment of boomerangs, bows and arrows, and canoe-paddles on the one hand and the
employment of tennis rackets, tug-of-war ropes, coins, stamps and words
on the other hand. The latter are instruments of interpersonal, i.e., con-
certed or competitive actions. Robinson Crusoe might play some games

of patience; but he could not play tennis or cricket. So a person who learns to use a tennis racket, a stroke-side oar, a coin or a word is inevitably in a position to notice other people using these things. He cannot master the tricks of such interpersonal transactions without at the same time finding out facts about some other people's employment and misemployment of them; and normally he will learn a good many of the tricks from noticing other people employing them. Even so, learning the knacks is not and does not require making a sociological study. A child may learn in the home and the village shop how to use pennies, shillings and pound notes; and his mastery of these slightly complex knacks is not improved by hearing how many people in other places and years have managed and now manage or mismanage their pennies, shillings and pound notes. Perfectly mastering a use is not getting to know everything, or even much, about a usage, even when mastering that use does causally involve finding out a bit about a few other people's practices. We were taught in the nursery how to handle a lot of words; but we were not being taught any historical or sociological generalities about employers of these words. That came later, if it came at all.

Before passing on we should notice one big difference between using canoe-paddles or tennis rackets on the one hand and using postage stamps, safety pins, coins and words on the other. Tennis rackets are wielded with greater or less skill; even the tennis champion studies to improve. But, with some unimportant reservations, it is true to say that coins, checks, stamps, separate words, buttons and shoelaces offer no scope for talent. Either a person knows or he does not know how to use and how not to misuse them. Of course literary composition and argumentation can be more or less skillful; but the essayist or lawyer does not know the meaning of "rabbit" or "and" better than Everyman. There is no room here for "better." Similarly, the champion chess player maneuvers more skillfully than the amateur; but he does not know the permitted moves of the pieces better. They both know them perfectly, or rather they just know them.

Certainly, the cultured chess player may describe the permitted moves better than does the uncultured chess player. But he does not make these moves any better. I give change for a half-crown no better than you do. We both just give the correct change. Yet I may describe such transactions more effectively than you can describe them. Knowing how to operate is not knowing how to tell how to operate. This point becomes important when we are discussing, say, the stock way (supposing there is one) of employing the word "cause." The doctor knows how to make this use of it as well as anyone, but he may not be able to answer any of the philosopher's inquiries about this way of using it.

In order to avoid these two big confusions, the confusion of "use" with "usefulness" and the confusion of "use" with "usage," I try nowadays to use, *inter alia,* "employ" and "employment" instead of the verb and noun "use." So I say this. Philosophers often have to try to describe the stock (or, more rarely, some nonstock) manner or way of employing an expression. Sometimes such an expression belongs to the vernacular; sometimes to some technical vocabulary; sometimes it is betwixt and between. Describing the mode of employment of an expression does not require and is not usually helped by information about the prevalence or unprevalence of this way of employing it. For the philosopher, like other folk, has long since learned how to employ or handle it, and what he is trying to describe is what he himself has learned.

Techniques are not vogues—but they may have vogues. Some of them must have vogues or be current in some other way. For it is no accident that ways of employing words, as of employing coins, stamps and chessmen, *tend* to be identical through a whole community and over a long stretch of time. We want to understand and be understood; and we learn our native tongue from our elders. Even without the pressure of legislation and dictionaries, our vocabularies tend towards uniformity. Fads and idiosyncrasies in these matters impair communication. Fads and idiosyncrasies in matters of postage stamps, coins and the moves of chessmen are ruled out by explicit legislation, and partly analogous conformities are imposed upon many technical vocabularies by such things as drill-manuals and textbooks. Notoriously these tendencies towards uniformity have their exceptions. However, as there naturally do exist many pretty widespread and pretty long-enduring vocabulary usages, it is sometimes condonable for a philosopher to remind his readers of a mode of employing an expression by alluding to "what everyone says" or "what no one says." The reader considers the mode of employment that he has long since learned and feels strengthened, when told that big battalions are on his side. In fact, of course, this appeal to prevalence is philosophically pointless, besides being philologically risky. What is wanted is, perhaps, the extraction of the logical rules implicitly governing a concept, i.e., a way of operating with an expression (or any other expression that does the same work). It is probable that the use of this expression, to perform this job, is widely current; but whether it is so or not is of no philosophical interest. Job-analysis is not Mass Observation. Nor is it helped by Mass Observation. But Mass Observation sometimes needs the aid of job-analysis.

Before terminating this discussion of the use of the expression "the use of the expression '. . . ,' " I want to draw attention to an interesting point. We can ask whether a person knows how to use and how not to misuse a certain word. But we cannot ask whether he knows how to use a certain *sentence.* When a block of words has congealed into a phrase we can ask whether he knows how to use the phrase. But when a sequence of words has not yet congealed into a phrase, while we can ask whether he knows how to use its ingredient words, we cannot easily ask whether he knows how to use that sequence. Why can we not even ask whether he knows how to use a certain sentence? For we talk about the meanings of sentences, seemingly just as we talk of the meanings of the words in it; so, if knowing the meaning of a word is knowing how to use it, we might have expected that knowing the meaning of a sentence was knowing how to use the sentence. Yet this glaringly does not go.

A cook uses salt, sugar, flour, beans and bacon in making a pie. She uses, and perhaps misuses, the ingredients. But she does not, in this way, use the pie. Her pie is not an ingredient. In a somewhat different way, the cook uses, and perhaps misuses, a rolling-pin, a fork, a frying-pan and an oven. These are the utensils with which she makes her pie. But the pie is not another utensil. The pie is (well or badly) composed out of the ingredients, by means of the utensils. It is what she used them for; but it cannot be listed in either class of them. Somewhat, but only somewhat, similarly a sentence is (well or badly) constructed out of words. It is what the speaker or writer uses them for. He composes it out of them. His sentence is not itself something which, in this way, he either uses or misuses, either uses or does not use. His composition is not a component of his composition. We can tell a person to say something (e.g., ask a question, give a command or narrate an anecdote), using a specified word or phrase; and he will know what he is being told to do. But if we just tell him to pronounce or write down, by itself, that specified word or phrase, he will see the difference between this order and the other one. For he is not now being told to use, i.e., *incorporate* the word or phrase, but only to pronounce it or write it down. Sentences are things that we say. Words and phrases are what we say things *with*.

There can be dictionaries of words and dictionaries of phrases. But there cannot be dictionaries of sentences. This is not because such dictionaries would have to be infinitely and therefore impracticably long. On the contrary, it is because they could not even begin. Words and phrases are there, in the bin, for people to avail themselves of when they want to say things. But the sayings of these things are not some more things which are there in the bin for people to avail themselves of, when they want to say these things. This fact that words and phrases can, while sentences cannot, be misused, since sentences cannot be, in this way, used at all, is quite consistent with the important fact that sentences can be well or ill constructed. We can say things awkwardly or ungrammatically and we can say things which are grammatically proper, but do not make sense.

It follows that there are some radical differences between what is meant by "the meaning of a word or phrase" and what is meant by "the meaning of a sentence." Understanding a word or phrase is knowing how to use it, i.e., make it perform its role in a wide range of sentences. But understanding a sentence is not knowing how to make it perform its role. The play has not got a role.

We are tempted to suppose that the question "How are word-meanings related to sentence-meanings?" is a tricky but genuine question, a question, perhaps, rather like "How is the purchasing power of my shilling related to the purchasing power of the contents of my pay-envelope?" But this model puts things awry from the start.

If I know the meaning of a word or phrase I know something like a body of unwritten rules, or something like an unwritten code or general recipe. I have learned to use the word correctly in an unlimited variety of different settings. What I know is, in this respect, somewhat like what I know when I know how to use a knight or a pawn at chess. I have learned to put it to its work anywhen and anywhere, if there is work for it to do. But the idea of putting a sentence to its work any-when and anywhere is fantastic. It has not got a role which it can per-form again and again in different plays. It has not got a role at all, any more than a play has a role. Knowing what it means is not knowing anything like a code or a body of rules, though it requires knowing the codes or rules governing the use of the words or phrases that make it up. There are general rules and recipes for constructing sentences of certain kinds; but not general rules or recipes for constructing the particular sentence "Today is Monday." Knowing the meaning of "Today is Monday" is not knowing general rules, codes or recipes governing the use of this sentence, since there is no such thing as the utilization or, therefore, the reutilization of this sentence. I expect that this ties up with the fact that sentences and clauses make sense or make no sense, where words neither do nor do not make sense, but only have meanings; and that pretense-sentences can be absurd or nonsensical, where pretense-words are neither absurd nor nonsensical, but only meaningless. I can say stupid things, but words can be neither stupid nor not stupid.

PHILOSOPHY AND ORDINARY LANGUAGE

The vogue of the phrase "the use of ordinary language" seems to suggest to some people the idea that there exists a philosophical doctrine according to which (1) all philosophical inquiries are concerned with vernacular, as opposed to more or less technical, academic or esoteric terms; and (2) in consequence, all philosophical discussions ought them-selves to be couched entirely in vernacular dictions. The inference is fallacious, though its conclusion has some truth in it. Even if it were true, which it is not, that all philosophical problems are concerned with nontechnical concepts, i.e., with the mode of employment of vernacular expressions, it would not follow from this (false) premise that the discussions of these problems must or had better be in jurymen's English, French or German.

From the fact that a philologist studies those English words which stem from Celtic roots, it does not follow that he must or had better say what he has to say about them in words of Celtic origin. From the fact that a psychologist is discussing the psychology of witticisms, it does not follow that he ought to write wittily all or any of the time. Clearly he ought not to write wittily most of the time.

Most philosophers have in fact employed a good number of the technical terms of past or contemporary logical theory. We may sometimes wish that they had taken a few more pinches of salt, but we do not reproach them for availing themselves of these technical expedients; we should have deplored their longwindedness if they had tried to do without them.

But enslavement to jargon, whether inherited or invented, is, certainly, a bad quality in any writer, whether he be a philosopher or not. It curtails the number of people who can understand and criticize his writings; so it tends to make his own thinking run in a private groove. The use of avoidable jargons is bad literary manners and bad pedagogic policy, as well as being detrimental to the thinker's own wits.

But this is not peculiar to philosophy. Bureaucrats, judges, theologians, literary critics, bankers and, perhaps above all, psychologists and sociologists would all be well advised to try very hard to write in plain and blunt words. Nonetheless, Hobbes who had this virtue of writing plainly and bluntly was a lesser philosopher than Kant who lacked it; and Plato's later dialogues, though harder to translate, have powers which his early dialogues are without. Nor is the simplicity of his diction in Mill's account of mathematics enough to make us prefer it to the account given by Frege, whose diction is more esoteric.

In short, there is no a priori or peculiar obligation laid upon philosophers to refrain from talking esoterically; but there is a general obligation upon all thinkers and writers to try to think and write both as powerfully and as plainly as possible. But plainness of diction and power of thought can vary independently, though it is not common for them to do so.

Incidentally it would be silly to require the language of professional journals to be as exoteric as the language of books. Colleagues can be expected to use and understand one another's terms of art. But books are not written only for colleagues. The judge should not address the jury in the language in which he may address his brother judges. Sometimes, but only sometimes, he may be well advised to address even his

brother judges, and himself, in the language in which he should address
the jury. It all depends on whether his technical terms are proving to
be a help or a hindrance. They are likely to be a hindrance when they
are legacies from a period in which today's questions were not even
envisaged. This is what justifies the regular and salutary rebellions of
philosophers against the philosophical jargons of their fathers.

There is another reason why philosophers ought sometimes to eschew
other people's technical terms. Even when a philosopher is interesting
himself in some of the cardinal concepts of, say, physical theory, he is
usually partly concerned to state the logical crossbearings between the
concepts of this theory and the concepts of mathematical, theological,
biological or psychological theory. Very often his radical puzzle is that
of determining these crossbearings. When trying to solve puzzles of this
sort, he cannot naïvely employ the dictions of either theory. He has to
stand back from both theories, and discuss the concepts of both in terms
which are proprietary to neither. He may coin neutral dictions of his
own, but for ease of understanding he may prefer the dictions of Everyman. These have this required neutrality, even if they lack that semi-
codification which disciplines the terms of art of professionalized thought.
Barter-terms are not as well regimented as the terms of the countinghouse; but when we have to determine rates of exchange betwen different
currencies, it is to barter-terms that we may have to turn. Intertheory
negotiations can be and may have to be conducted in pre-theory dictions.

So far I have, I hope, been mollifying rather than provoking. I now
want to say two philosophically contentious things.

1. There is a special reason why philosophers, unlike other profes-
sionals and specialists, are constantly jettisoning in toto all the technical
terms of their own predecessors (save some of the technical terms of
formal logic); i.e., why the jargon words of epistemology, ethics,
aesthetics, etc., seem to be half-hardy annuals rather than hardy peren-
nials. The reason is this. The experts who use the technical terms of
bridge, law, chemistry and plumbing learn to employ these terms partly
from official instructions but largely by directly engaging in the special
techniques and by directly dealing with the special materials or objects
of their specialism. They familiarize themselves with the harness by
having to drive their (to us unfamiliar) horses.

But the terms of art of philosophy itself (save for those of formal
logic) are not like this. There is no peculiar field of knowledge or adept-
ness in which philosophers ex officio make themselves the experts—except
of course the business of philosophizing itself. We know by what special
sorts of work mastery is acquired of the concepts of *finesse, tort, sul-
fanilamide* and *valve-seating*. But by what corresponding special sorts
of work do philosophers get their supposed corresponding mastery of

the concepts of *Cognition, Sensation, Secondary Qualities,* and *Essences*? What exercises and predicaments have forced them to learn just how to use and how not to misuse these terms?

Philosophers' arguments which turn on these terms are apt, sooner or later, to start to rotate idly. There is nothing to make them point north rather than nor'-nor'-east. The bridge player cannot play fast and loose with the concepts of *finesse* and *revoke.* If he tries to make them work in a way palatable to him, they jib. The unofficial terms of everyday discourse are like the official terms of specialisms in this important respect. They too jib, if maltreated. It is no more possible to say that someone knows something to be the case which is not so than it is possible to say that the player of the first card in a game of bridge has revoked. We have had to learn in the hard school of daily life how to deploy the verb "know"; and we have had to learn at the bridge table how to deploy the verb "revoke." There is no such hard school in which to learn how to deploy the verbs "cognize" and "sense." These go through what motions we care to require of them, which means that they have acquired no discipline of their own at all. So the philosophical arguments, which are supposed to deploy these units, win and lose no fights, since these units have no fight in them. Hence, the appeal from philosophical jargon to the expressions which we have all had to learn to use properly (as the chess player has had to learn the moves of his pieces) is often one well worth making; where a corresponding appeal to the vocabulary of Everyman from the official parlance of a science, of a game or of law would often, not always, be ridiculous. One contrast of "ordinary" (in the phrase "ordinary language") is with "philosophers' jargon."

2. But now for quite a different point and one of considerable contemporary importance. The appeal to what we do and do not say, or can and cannot say, is often stoutly resisted by the protagonists of one special doctrine, and stoutly pressed by its antagonists. This doctrine is the doctrine that philosophical disputes can and should be settled by formalizing the warring theses. A theory is formalized when it is translated out of the natural language (untechnical, technical or semi-technical), in which it was originally excogitated, into a deliberately constructed notation, the notation, perhaps, of *Principia Mathematica.* The logic of a theoretical position can, it is claimed, be regularized by stretching its nonformal concepts between the topic-neutral logical constants whose conduct in inferences is regulated by set drills. Formalization will replace logical perplexities by logical problems amenable to known and teachable procedures of calculation. Thus one contrast of "ordinary" (in the phrase "ordinary language") is with "notational."

Of those to whom this, the formalizer's dream, appears a mere dream (I am one of them), some maintain that the logic of everyday statements and even the logic of the statements of scientists, lawyers, historians and bridge players cannot in principle be adequately represented by the formulas of formal logic. The so-called logical constants do indeed have, partly by deliberate prescription, their scheduled logical powers; but the nonformal expressions both of everyday discourse and of technical discourse have their own unscheduled logical powers, and these are not reducible without remainder to those of the carefully wired marionettes of formal logic. The title of a novel by A. E. W. Mason, "They Wouldn't Be Chessmen," applies well to both the technical and the untechnical expressions of professional and daily life. This is not to say that the examination of the logical behavior of the terms of nonnotational discourse is not assisted by studies in formal logic. Of course it is. So may chess playing assist generals, though waging campaigns cannot be replaced by playing games of chess.

I do not want here to thrash out this important issue. I want only to show that resistance to one sort of appeal to ordinary language ought to involve championing the program of formalization. "Back to ordinary language" can be (but often is not) the slogan of those who have awakened from the formalizer's dream. This slogan, so used, should be repudiated only by those who hope to replace philosophizing by reckoning.

VERDICT

Well, then, has philosophy got something to do with the use of expressions or hasn't it? To ask this is simply to ask whether conceptual discussions, i.e., discussions about the concept of, say, *voluntariness, infinitesimals, number* or *cause,* come under the heading of philosophical discussions. Of course they do. They always have done, and they have not stopped doing so now.

Whether we gain more than we lose by sedulously advertising the fact that what we are investigating is the stock way of operating with, say, the word "cause," depends a good deal on the context of the discussions and the intellectual habits of the people with whom we are discussing it. It is certainly a longwinded way of announcing what we are doing; and inverted commas are certainly vexatious to the eye. But, more important than these nuisances, preoccupation with questions about methods tends to distract us from prosecuting the methods themselves. We run, as a rule, worse, not better, if we think a lot about our feet. So let us, at least on alternate days, speak instead of investigating the concept of *causation.* Or, better still, let us, on those days, not speak of it at all but just do it.

But the more longwinded idiom has some big compensating advantages. If we are inquiring into problems of perception, i.e., discussing questions about the concepts of seeing, hearing and smelling, we may be taken to be tackling the questions of opticians, neurophysiologists or psychologists, and even fall into this mistake ourselves. It is then salutary to keep on reminding ourselves and one another that what we are after is accounts of how certain words work, namely words like "see," "look," "overlook," "blind," "visualize" and lots of other affiliated expressions.

One last point. I have talked in general terms about learning and describing the modes of employment of expressions. But there are many different dimensions of these modes, only some of which are of interest to philosophers. Differences of stylistic elegance, rhetorical persuasiveness, and social propriety need to be considered, but not, save *per accidens,* by philosophers. Churchill would have made a rhetorical blunder if he had said, instead of "We shall fight them on the beaches . . . ," "We shall fight them on the sands. . . ." "Sands" would have raised thoughts of children's holidays at Skegness. But this kind of misemployment of "sands" is not the kind of mishandling that interests us. We are interested in the informal logic of the employment of expressions, the nature of the logical howlers that people do or might commit if they strung their words together in certain ways, or, more positively, in the logical force that expressions have as components of theories and as pivots of concrete arguments. That is why, in our discussions, we argue *with* expressions and *about* those expressions in one and the same breath. We are trying to register what we are exhibiting; to codify the very logical codes which we are then and there observing.

A PLEA FOR EXCUSES

J. L. AUSTIN

The subject of this paper, *Excuses,* is one not to be treated, but only to be introduced, within such limits. It is, or might be, the name of a whole branch, even a ramiculated branch, of philosophy, or at least of one fashion of philosophy. I shall try, therefore, first to state *what* the subject is, *why* it is worth studying, and *how* it may be studied, all this at a regrettably lofty level: and then I shall illustrate, in more congenial but desultory detail, some of the methods to be used, together with their limitations, and some of the unexpected results to be expected and lessons to be learned. Much, of course, of the amusement, and of the instruction, comes in drawing the coverts of the microglot, in hounding down the minutiae, and to this I can do no more here than incite you. But I owe it to the subject to say, that it has long afforded me what philosophy is so often thought, and made, barren of—the fun of dis-

"The Presidential Address to the Aristotelian Society, 1956," Proceedings of the Aristotelian Society, 1956-1957, *Vol. LVII; reprinted in J. L. Austin,* Philosophical Papers *(Oxford: The Clarendon Press, 1961). Reprinted by permission of Mrs. Austin, The Clarendon Press, and the editor of the Aristotelian Society.*

covery, the pleasures of cooperation, and the satisfaction of reaching agreement.

What, then, is the subject? I am here using the word "excuses" *for a title,* but it would be unwise to freeze too fast to this one noun and its partner verb: indeed for some time I used to use "extenuation" instead. Still, on the whole "excuses" is probably the most central and embracing term in the field, although this includes others of importance—"plea," "defense," "justification," and so on. When, then, do we "excuse" conduct, our own or somebody else's? When are "excuses" proffered?

In general, the situation is one where someone is *accused* of having done something, or (if that will keep it any cleaner) where someone is *said* to have done something which is bad, wrong, inept, unwelcome, or in some other of the numerous possible ways untoward. Thereupon he, or someone on his behalf, will try to defend his conduct or to get him out of it.

One way of going about this is to admit flatly that he, X, did do that very thing, A, but to argue that it was a good thing, or the right or sensible thing, or a permissible thing to do, either in general or at least in the special circumstances of the occasion. To take this line is to *justify* the action, to give reasons for doing it: not to say, to brazen it out, to glory in it, or the like.

A different way of going about it is to admit that it wasn't a good thing to have done, but to argue that it is not quite fair or correct to say *baldly* "X did A." We may say it isn't fair just to say X did it; perhaps he was under somebody's influence, or was nudged. Or, it isn't fair to say baldly he *did* A; it may have been partly accidental, or an unintentional slip. Or, it isn't fair to say he did simply A—he was really doing something quite different and A was only incidental, or he was looking at the whole thing quite differently. Naturally these arguments can be combined or overlap or run into each other.

In the one defense, briefly, we accept responsibility but deny that it was bad: in the other, we admit that it was bad but don't accept full, or even any, responsibility.

By and large, justifications can be kept distinct from excuses, and I shall not be so anxious to talk about them because they have enjoyed more than their fair share of philosophical attention. But the two certainly can be confused, and can *seem* to go very near to each other, even if they do not perhaps actually do so. You dropped the tea tray: Certainly, but an emotional storm was about to break out: or, Yes, but there was a wasp. In each case the defense, very soundly, insists on a fuller description of the event in its context; but the first is a justification, the second an excuse. Again, if the objection is to the use of such a dyslogistic verb as "murdered," this may be on the ground that the killing was done in battle (justification) or on the ground that it was only accidental if reckless (excuse). It is arguable that we do not use the terms "justification" and "excuse" as carefully as we might; a miscellany of even less-clear terms, such as "extenuation," "palliation," "mitigation," hovers uneasily between partial justification and partial excuse; and when we plead, say, provocation, there is genuine uncertainty or ambiguity as to what we mean—is *he* partly responsible, because he roused a violent impulse or passion in me, so that it wasn't truly or merely me acting "of my own accord" (excuse)? Or is it rather that, he having done me such injury, I was entitled to retaliate (justification)? Such doubts merely make it the more urgent to clear up the usage of these various terms. But that the defenses I have for convenience labeled "justification" and "excuse" are in principle distinct can scarcely be doubted.

This then is the sort of situation we have to consider under "excuses." I will only further point out how very wide a field it covers. We have, of course, to bring in the opposite numbers of excuses—the expressions that *aggravate,* such as "deliberately," "on purpose," and so on, if only for the reason that an excuse often takes the form of a rebuttal of one of these. But we have also to bring in a large number of expressions which at first blush look not so much like excuses as like accusations—"clumsiness," "tactlessness," "thoughtlessness," and the like. Because it has always to be remembered that few excuses get us out of it *completely*: the average excuse, in a poor situation, gets us only out of the fire into the frying-pan—but still, of course, any frying-pan in a fire. If I have broken your dish or your romance, maybe the best defense I can find will be clumsiness.

Why, if this is what "excuses" are, should we trouble to investigate them? It might be thought reason enough that their production has always bulked so large among human activities. But to moral philosophy in particular a study of them will contribute in special ways, both positively towards the development of a cautious, latter-day version of conduct, and negatively towards the correction of older and hastier theories.

In ethics we study, I suppose, the good and the bad, the right and the wrong, and this must be for the most part in some connection with conduct or the doing of actions. Yet before we consider what actions are good or bad, right or wrong, it is proper to consider first what is meant by, and what not, and what is included under, and what not, the expression "doing an action" or "doing something." These are expressions still too little examined on their own account and merits, just as the general notion of "saying something" is still too lightly passed over in logic. There is indeed a vague and comforting idea in the background that, after all, in the last analysis, doing an action must come down to the making of physical movements with parts of the body; but this is about as true as that saying something must, in the last analysis, come down to making movements of the tongue.

The beginning of sense, not to say wisdom, is to realize that "doing an action," as used in philosophy,[1] is a highly abstract expression—it is a stand-in used in the place of any (or almost any?) verb with a personal subject, in the same sort of way that "thing" is a stand-in for any (or when we remember, almost any) noun substantive, and "quality" a stand-in for the adjective. Nobody, to be sure, relies on such dummies quite implicitly quite indefinitely. Yet notoriously it is possible to arrive at, or to derive the idea for, an oversimplified metaphysics from the obsession with "things" and their "qualities." In a similar way, less commonly recognized even in these semi-sophisticated times, we fall for the myth of the verb. We treat the expression "doing an action" no longer as a stand-in for a verb with a personal subject, as which it has no doubt some uses, and might have more if the range of verbs were not left unspecified, but as a self-explanatory, ground-level description, one which brings adequately into the open the essential features of everything that comes, by simple inspection, under it. We scarcely notice even the most patent exceptions or difficulties (is to think something, or to say something, or to try to do something, to do an action?), any more than we fret, in the *ivresse des grandes profondeurs,* as to whether flames are things or events. So we come easily to think of our behavior over any time, and of a life as a whole, as consisting in doing now action A, next action B, then action C, and so on, just as elsewhere we come to think of the world as consisting of this, that, and the other substance or material thing, each with its properties. All "actions" are, as actions (meaning what?), equal, composing a quarrel with striking a match, winning a war with sneezing: worse still, we assimilate them one and all to the supposedly most obvious and easy cases, such as posting letters or moving fingers, just as we assimilate all "things" to horses or beds.

If we are to continue to use this expression in sober philosophy, we need to ask such questions as: Is to sneeze to do an action? Or is to breathe, or to see, or to checkmate, or each one of countless others? In short, for what range of verbs, as used on what occasions, is "doing an action" a stand-in? What have they in common, and what do those excluded severally lack? Again we need to ask how we decide what is the correct name for "the" action that somebody did—and what, indeed, are the rules for the use of "the" action, "an" action, "one" action, a "part" or "phase" of an action and the like. Further, we need

---

[1] This use has little to do with the more down-to-earth occurrences of "action" in ordinary speech.

to realize that even the "simplest" named actions are not so simple—certainly are not the mere makings of physical movements, and to ask what more, then, comes in (intentions? conventions?) and what does not (motives?), and what is the detail of the complicated internal machinery we use in "acting"—the receipt of intelligence, the appreciation of the situation, the invocation of principles, the planning, the control of execution and the rest.

In two main ways the study of excuses can throw light on these fundamental matters. First, to examine excuses is to examine cases where there has been some abnormality or failure: and as so often, the abnormal will throw light on the normal, will help us to penetrate the blinding veil of ease and obviousness that hides the mechanisms of the natural successful act. It rapidly becomes plain that the breakdowns signalized by the various excuses are of radically different kinds, affecting different parts or stages of the machinery, which the excuses consequently pick out and sort out for us. Further, it emerges that not *every* slip-up occurs in connection with *every*thing that could be called an "action," that not every excuse is apt with every verb—far indeed from it: and this provides us with one means of introducing some classification into the vast miscellany of "actions." If we classify them according to the particular selection of breakdowns to which each is liable, this should assign them their places in some family group or groups of actions, or in some model of the machinery of acting.

In this sort of way, the philosophical study of conduct can get off to a positive fresh start. But by the way, and more negatively, a number of traditional cruces or mistakes in this field can be resolved or removed. First among these comes the problem of Freedom. While it has been the tradition to present this as the "positive" term requiring elucidation, there is little doubt that to say we acted "freely" (in the philosopher's use, which is only faintly related to the everyday use) is to say only that we acted *not* unfreely, in one or another of the many heterogeneous ways of so acting (under duress, or what not). Like "real," "free" is only used to rule out the suggestion of some or all of its recognized antitheses. As "truth" is not a name for a characteristic of assertions, so "freedom" is not a name for a characteristic of actions, but the name of a dimension in which actions are assessed. In examining all the ways in which each action may not be "free," i.e., the cases in which it will not do to say simply "X did A," we may hope to dispose of the problem of Freedom. Aristotle has often been chidden for talking about excuses or pleas and overlooking "the real problem": in my own case, it was when I began to see the injustice of this charge that I first became interested in excuses.

There is much to be said for the view that, philosophical tradition apart, Responsibility would be a better candidate for the role here assigned to Freedom. If ordinary language is to be our guide, it is to evade responsibility, or full responsibility, that we most often make excuses, and I have used the word myself in this way above. But in fact "responsibility" too seems not really apt in all cases: I do not exactly evade responsibility when I plead clumsiness or tactlessness, nor, often, when I plead that I only did it unwillingly or reluctantly, and still less if I plead that I had in the circumstances no choice: here I was constrained and have an excuse (or justification), yet may accept responsibility. It may be, then, that at least two key terms, Freedom and Responsibility, are needed: the relation between them is not clear, and it may be hoped that the investigation of excuses will contribute towards its clarification.[2]

So much, then, for ways in which the study of excuses may throw light on ethics. But there are also reasons why it is an attractive subject methodologically, at least if we are to proceed from "ordinary language," that is, by examining *what we should say when,* and so why and what we should mean by it. Perhaps this method, at least as *one* philosophical method, scarcely requires justification at present—too evidently, there is gold in them thar hills: more opportune would be a warning about the care and thoroughness needed if it is not to fall into disrepute. I will, however, justify it very briefly.

First, words are our tools, and, as a minimum, we should use clean tools: we should know what we mean and what we do not, and we must forearm ourselves against the traps that language sets us. Secondly, words are not (except in their own little corner) facts or things: we need therefore to prize them off the world, to hold them apart from and against it, so that we can realize their inadequacies and arbitrariness, and can relook at the world without blinkers. Thirdly, and more hopefully, our common stock of words embodies all the distinctions men have found worth drawing, and the connections they have found worth marking, in the lifetimes of many generations: these surely are likely to be more numerous, more sound, since they have stood up to the long test of the survival of the fittest, and more subtle, at least in all ordinary and reasonably practical matters, than any that you or I are likely to think up in our armchairs of an afternoon—the most favored alternative method.

---

[2] Another well-flogged horse in these same stakes is Blame. At least two things seem confused together under this term. Sometimes when I blame X for doing A, say for breaking the vase, it is a question simply or mainly of my disapproval of A, breaking the vase, which unquestionably X did: but sometimes it is, rather, a question simply or mainly of how far I think X responsible for A, which unquestionably was bad. Hence if somebody says he blames me for something, I may answer by giving a *justification,* so that he will cease to disapprove of what I did, or else by giving an *excuse,* so that he will cease to hold me, at least entirely and in every way, responsible for doing it.

In view of the prevalence of the slogan "ordinary language," and of such names as "linguistic" or "analytic" philosophy or "the analysis of language," one thing needs specially emphasizing to counter misunderstandings. When we examine what we should say when, what words we should use in what situations, we are looking again not *merely* at words (or "meanings," whatever they may be) but also at the realities we use the words to talk about: we are using a sharpened awareness of words to sharpen our perception of, though not as the final arbiter of, the phenomena. For this reason I think it might be better to use, for this way of doing philosophy, some less misleading name than those given above— for instance, "linguistic phenomenology," only that is rather a mouthful.

Using, then, such a method, it is plainly preferable to investigate a field where ordinary language is rich and subtle, as it is in the pressingly practical matter of Excuses, but certainly is not in the matter, say, of Time. At the same time we should prefer a field which is not too much trodden into bogs or tracks by traditional philosophy, for in that case even "ordinary" language will often have become infected with the jargon of extinct theories, and our own prejudices too, as the upholders or imbibers of theoretical views, will be too readily, and often insensibly, engaged. Here too, Excuses form an admirable topic; we can discuss at least clumsiness, or absence of mind, or inconsiderateness, even spontaneousness, without remembering what Kant thought, and so progress by degrees even to discussing deliberation without for once remembering Aristotle or self-control without Plato. Granted that our subject is, as already claimed for it, neighboring, analogous, or germane in some way to some notorious center of philosophical trouble, then, with these two further requirements satisfied, we should be certain of what we are after: a good site for *field work* in philosophy. Here at last we should be able to unfreeze, to loosen up and get going on agreeing about discoveries, however small, and on agreeing about how to reach agreement.[3] How much it is to be wished that similar field work will soon be undertaken in, say, aesthetics; if only we could forget for a while about the beautiful and get down instead to the dainty and the dumpy.

There are, I know, or are supposed to be, snags in "linguistic" philosophy, which those not very familiar with it find, sometimes not without glee or relief, daunting. But with snags, as with nettles, the thing to do is to grasp them—and to climb above them. I will mention two in particular, over which the study of excuses may help to encourage us. The first is the snag of Loose (or Divergent or Alternative) Usage; and the second the crux of the Last Word. Do we all say the same,

---

[3] All of which was seen and claimed by Socrates, when he first betook himself to the way of Words.

and only the same, things in the same situations? Don't usages differ? And, Why should what we all ordinarily say be the only or the best or final way of putting it? Why should it even be true?

Well, people's usages do vary, and we do talk loosely, and we do say different things apparently indifferently. But first, not nearly as much as one would think. When we come down to cases, it transpires in the very great majority that what we had thought was our wanting to say different things of and in *the same* situation was really not so—we had simply imagined the situation *slightly* differently: which is all too easy to do, because of course no situation (and we are dealing with *imagined* situations) is ever "completely" described. The more we imagine the situation in detail, with a background of story—and it is worth employing the most idiosyncratic or, sometimes, boring means to stimulate and to discipline our wretched imaginations—the less we find we disagree about what we should say. Nevertheless, *sometimes* we do ultimately disagree: sometimes we must allow a usage to be, though appalling, yet actual; sometimes we should genuinely use either or both of two different descriptions. But why should this daunt us? All that is happening is entirely explicable. If our usages disagree, then you use "X" where I use "Y," or more probably (and more intriguingly) your conceptual system is different from mine, though very likely it is at least equally consistent and serviceable: in short, we can find *why* we disagree—you choose to classify in one way, I in another. If the usage is loose, we can understand the temptation that leads to it, and the distinctions that it blurs: if there are "alternative" descriptions, then the situation can be described or can be "structured" in two ways, or perhaps it is one where, for current purposes, the two alternatives come down to the same. A disagreement as to what we should say is not to be shied off, but to be pounced upon: for the explanation of it can hardly fail to be illuminating. If we light on an electron that rotates the wrong way, that is a discovery, a portent to be followed up, not a reason for chucking physics: and by the same token, a genuinely loose or eccentric talker is a rare specimen to be prized.

As practice in learning to handle this bogey, in learning the essential *rubrics,* we could scarcely hope for a more promising exercise than the study of excuses. Here, surely, is just the sort of situation where people will say "almost anything," because they are so flurried, or so anxious to get off. "It was a mistake," "It was an accident"—how readily these can *appear* indifferent, and even be used together. Yet, a story or two, and everybody will not merely agree that they are completely different, but even discover for himself what the difference is and what each means.[4]

---

[4] You have a donkey, so have I, and they graze in the same field. The day comes when I conceive a dislike for mine. I go to shoot it, draw a bead on it,

Then, for the Last Word. Certainly ordinary language has no claim
to be the last word, if there is such a thing. It embodies, indeed, something better than the metaphysics of the Stone Age, namely, as was said,
the inherited experience and acumen of many generations of men. But
then, that acumen has been concentrated primarily upon the practical
business of life. If a distinction works well for practical purposes in
ordinary life (no mean feat, for even ordinary life is full of hard cases),
then there is sure to be something in it, it will not mark nothing: yet this
is likely enough to be not the best way of arranging things if our interests are more extensive or intellectual than the ordinary. And again,
that experience has been derived only from the sources available to
ordinary men throughout most of civilized history: it has not been fed
from the resources of the microscope and its successors. And it must
be added too, that superstition and error and fantasy of all kinds do
become incorporated in ordinary language and even sometimes stand up
to the survival test (only, when they do, why should we not detect it?).
Certainly, then, ordinary language is *not* the last word: in principle it
can everywhere be supplemented and improved upon and superseded.
Only remember, it *is* the *first* word.[5]

For this problem too the field of Excuses is a fruitful one. Here is
matter both contentious and practically important for everybody, so that
ordinary language is on its toes: yet also, on its back it has long had a
bigger flea to bite it, in the shape of the Law, and both again have lately
attracted the attentions of yet another, and at least a healthily growing,
flea, in the shape of psychology. In the law a constant stream of actual
cases, more novel and more tortuous than the mere imagination could
contrive, are brought up *for decision*—that is, formulas for docketing
them must somehow be found. Hence it is necessary first to be careful
with, but also to be brutal with, to torture, to fake, and to override,
ordinary language: we cannot here evade or forget the whole affair.
(In ordinary life we dismiss the puzzles that crop up about time, but
we cannot do that indefinitely in physics.) Psychology likewise produces
novel cases, but it also produces new methods for bringing phenomena
under observation and study: moreover, unlike the law, it has an un-
biased interest in the totality of them and is unpressed for decision.
Hence its own special and constant need to supplement, to revise and

---

fire: the brute falls in its tracks. I inspect the victim, and find to my horror that
it is *your* donkey. I appear on your doorstep with the remains and say—what?
"I say, old sport, I'm awfully sorry, etc., I've shot your donkey *by accident*"*?*
Or *"by mistake"?* Then again, I go to shoot my donkey as before, draw a bead
on it, fire—but as I do so, the beasts move, and to my horror yours falls.
Again the scene on the doorstep—what do I say? "By mistake"? Or "by accident"?

[5] And forget, for once and for a while, that other curious question "Is it
true?" May we?

to supersede the classifications of both ordinary life and the law. We have, then, ample material for practice in learning to handle the bogey of the Last Word, however it should be handled.

Suppose, then, that we set out to investigate excuses, what are the methods and resources initially available? Our object is to imagine the varieties of situation in which we make excuses, and to examine the expressions used in making them. If we have a lively imagination, together perhaps with an ample experience of dereliction, we shall go far, only we need system: I do not know how many of you keep a list of the kinds of fool you make of yourselves. It is advisable to use systematic aids, of which there would appear to be three at least. I list them here in order of availability to the layman.

First we may use the dictionary—quite a concise one will do, but the use must be *thorough*. Two methods suggest themselves, both a little tedious, but repaying. One is to read the book through, listing all the words that seem relevant; this does not take as long as many suppose. The other is to start with a widish selection of obviously relevant terms, and to consult the dictionary under each: it will be found that, in the explanations of the various meanings of each, a surprising number of other terms occur, which are germane though of course not often synonymous. We then look up each of *these*, bringing in more for our bag from the "definitions" given in each case; and when we have continued for a little, it will generally be found that the family circle begins to close, until ultimately it is complete and we come only upon repetitions. This method has the advantage of grouping the terms into convenient clusters —but of course a good deal will depend upon the comprehensiveness of our initial selection.

Working the dictionary, it is interesting to find that a high percentage of the terms connected with excuses prove to be *adverbs*, a type of word which has not enjoyed so large a share of the philosophical limelight as the noun, substantive or adjective, and the verb: this is natural because, as was said, the tenor of so many excuses is that I did it but only *in a way*, not just flatly like that—i.e., the verb needs modifying. Besides adverbs, however, there are other words of all kinds, including numerous abstract nouns, "misconception," "accident," "purpose," and the like, and a few verbs too, which often hold key positions for the grouping of excuses into classes at a high level ("couldn't help," "didn't mean to," "didn't realize," or again "intend," and "attempt"). In connection with the nouns another neglected class of words is prominent, namely, prepositions. Not merely does it matter considerably which preposition, often of several, is being used with a given substantive, but further the prepositions deserve study on their own account. For the question suggests itself, Why are the nouns in one group governed by "under," in another by "on," in yet another by "by" or "through" or "from" or "for" or "with," and so on? It will be disappointing if there prove to be no good reasons for such groupings.

Our second sourcebook will naturally be the law. This will provide us with an immense miscellany of untoward cases, and also with a useful list of recognized pleas, together with a good deal of acute analysis of both. No one who tries this resource will long be in doubt, I think, that the common law, and in particular the law of tort, is the richest storehouse; crime and contract contribute some special additions of their own, but tort is altogether more comprehensive and more flexible. But even here, and still more with so old and hardened a branch of the law as crime, much caution is needed with the arguments of counsel and the dicta or decisions of judges: acute though these are, it has always to be remembered that, in legal cases, (1) there is the overriding requirement that a decision be reached, and a relatively black or white decision— guilty or not guilty—for the plaintiff or for the defendant; (2) there is the general requirement that the charge or action and the pleadings be brought under one or another of the heads and procedures that have come in the course of history to be accepted by the courts (These, though fairly numerous, are still few and stereotyped in comparison with the accusations and defenses of daily life. Moreover contentions of many kinds are beneath the law, as too trivial, or outside it, as too purely moral—for example, inconsiderateness); (3) there is the general requirement that we argue from and abide by precedents (The value of this in the law is unquestionable, but it can certainly lead to distortions of ordinary beliefs and expressions). For such reasons as these, obviously closely connected and stemming from the nature and function of the law, practicing lawyers and jurists are by no means so careful as they might be to give to our ordinary expressions their ordinary meanings and applications. There is special pleading and evasion, stretching and strait-jacketing, besides the invention of technical terms, or technical senses for common terms. Nevertheless, it is a perpetual and salutary surprise to discover how much is to be learned from the law; and it is to be added that if a distinction drawn is a sound one, even though not yet recognized in law, a lawyer can be relied upon to take note of it, for it may be dangerous not to—if he does not, his opponent may.

Finally, the third sourcebook is psychology, with which I include such studies as anthropology and animal behavior. Here I speak with even more trepidation than about the Law. But this at least is clear, that some varieties of behavior, some ways of acting or explanations of the doing of actions, are here noticed and classified which have not been observed or named by ordinary men and hallowed by ordinary language, though perhaps they often might have been so if they had been of more practical importance. There is real danger in contempt for the "jargon" of psychology, at least when it sets out to supplement, and at least sometimes when it sets out to supplant, the language of ordinary life.

With these sources, and with the aid of the imagination, it will go hard if we cannot arrive at the meanings of large numbers of expressions and at the understanding and classification of large numbers of "actions." Then we shall comprehend clearly much that, before, we only made use of *ad hoc*. Definition, I would add, explanatory definition, should stand high among our aims: it is not enough to show how clever we are by showing how obscure everything is. Clarity, too, I know, has been said to be not enough: but perhaps it will be time to go into that when we are within measurable distance of achieving clarity on some matter.

So much for the cackle. It remains to make a few remarks, not, I am afraid, in any very coherent order, about the types of significant result to be obtained and the more general lessons to be learned from the study of Excuses.

1. *No modification without aberration.* When it is stated that X did A, there is a temptation to suppose that given some, indeed perhaps *any,* expression modifying the verb we shall be entitled to insert either it or its opposite or negation in our statement: that is, we shall be entitled to ask, typically, "Did X do A Mly or not Mly?" (e.g., "Did X murder Y voluntarily or involuntarily?"), and to answer one or the other. Or as a minimum it is supposed that if X did A there must be at least *one* modifying expression that we could, justifiably and informatively, insert with the verb. In the great majority of cases of the use of the great majority of verbs ("murder" perhaps is not one of the majority) such suppositions are quite unjustified. The natural economy of language dictates that for the *standard* case covered by any normal verb—not, perhaps, a verb of omen such as "murder," but a verb like "eat" or "kick" or "croquet"—no modifying expression is required or even permissible. Only if we do the action named in some *special* way or circumstances, different from those in which such an act is naturally done (and of course both the normal and the abnormal differ according to what verb in particular is in question), is a modifying expression called for, or even in order. I sit in my chair, in the usual way—I am not in a daze or influenced by threats or the like: here, it will not do to say either that I sat in it intentionally or that I did not sit in it intentionally,[6] nor yet that I sat in it automatically or from habit or what you will. It is bedtime, I am alone, I yawn: but I do not yawn invol-

---

[6] Caveat or hedge: of course we can say "I did *not* sit in it 'intentionally' " as a way simply of repudiating the suggestion that I sat in it intentionally.

untarily (or voluntarily!), nor yet deliberately. To yawn in any such peculiar way is just not to just yawn.

2. *Limitation of application.* Expressions modifying verbs, typically adverbs, have limited ranges of application. That is, given any adverb of excuse, such as "unwittingly" or "spontaneously" or "impulsively," it will not be found that it makes good sense to attach it to any and every verb of "action" in any and every context: indeed, it will often apply only to a comparatively narrow range of such verbs. Something in the lad's upturned face appealed to him, he threw a brick at it—"spontaneously"? The interest then is to discover why some actions can be excused in a particular way but not others, particularly perhaps the latter.[7] This will largely elucidate the meaning of the excuse, and at the same time will illuminate the characteristics typical of the group of "actions" it picks out: very often too it will throw light on some detail of the machinery of "action" in general (see 4), or on our standards of acceptable conduct (see 5). It is specially important in the case of some of the terms most favored by philosophers or jurists to realize that at least in ordinary speech (disregarding backseepage of jargon) they are not used so universally or so dichotomistically. For example, take "voluntarily" and "involuntarily": we may join the army or make a gift voluntarily, we may hiccough or make a small gesture involuntarily, and the more we consider further actions which we might naturally be said to do in either of these ways, the more circumscribed and unlike each other do the two classes become, until we even doubt whether there is *any* verb with which both adverbs are equally in place. Perhaps there are some such; but at least sometimes when we may think we have found one it is an illusion, an apparent exception that really does prove the rule. I can perhaps "break a cup" voluntarily, *if* that is done, say, as an act of self-impoverishment: and I can perhaps break another involuntarily, *if,* say, I make an involuntary movement which breaks it. Here, plainly, the two acts described each as "breaking a cup" are really very different, and the one is similar to acts typical of the "voluntary" class, the other to acts typical of the "involuntary" class.

3. *The importance of Negations and Opposites.* "Voluntarily" and "involuntarily," then, are not opposed in the obvious sort of way that they are made to be in philosophy or jurisprudence. The "opposite," or rather "opposites," of "voluntarily" might be "under constraint" of some sort, duress or obligation or influence;[8] the opposite of "involuntarily" might be "deliberately" or "on purpose" or the like. Such diver-

---

[7] For we are sometimes not so good at observing what we *can't* say as what we can, yet the first is pretty regularly the more revealing.

[8] But remember, when I sign a check in the normal way, I do *not* do so *either* "voluntarily" *or* "under constraint."

gences in opposites indicate that "voluntarily" and "involuntarily," in spite of their apparent connection, are fish from very different kettles. In general, it will pay us to take nothing for granted or as obvious about negations and opposites. It does not pay to assume that a word must have an opposite, or one opposite, whether it is a "positive" word like "wilfully" or a "negative" word like "inadvertently." Rather, we should be asking ourselves such questions as why there is no use for the adverb "advertently." For above all it will not do to assume that the "positive" word must be around to wear the trousers; commonly enough the "negative" (looking) word marks the (positive) abnormality, while the "positive" word, *if* it exists, merely serves to rule out the suggestion of that abnormality. It is natural enough, in view of what was said in (1) above, for the "positive" word not to be found at all in some cases. I do an act A_1 (say, crush a snail) *inadvertently* if, in the course of executing by means of movements of my bodily parts some other act A_2 (say, in walking down the public path), I fail to exercise such meticulous supervision over the courses of those movements as would have been needed to ensure that they did not bring about the untoward event (here, the impact on the snail).[9] By claiming that A_1 was inadvertent we place it, where we imply it belongs, on this special level, in a class of incidental happenings which must occur in the doing of any physical act. To lift the act out of this class, we need and possess the expression "not . . . inadvertently": "advertently," if used for this purpose, would suggest that, if the act was not done inadvertently, then it must have been done noticing what I was doing, which is far from necessarily the case (e.g., if I did it absent-mindedly), or at least that there is *something* in common to the ways of doing all acts not done inadvertently, which is not the case. Again, there is no use for "advertently" at the *same* level as "inadvertently": in passing the butter I do not knock over the cream-jug, though I do (inadvertently) knock over the teacup—yet I do not by-pass the cream-jug *advertently*: for at this level, below supervision in detail, *anything* that we do is, if you like, inadvertent, though we only call it so, and indeed only call it something we have done, if there is something untoward about it.

A further point of interest in studying so-called "negative" terms is the manner of their formation. Why are the words in one group formed

---

[9] Or analogously: I do an act A_1 (say, divulge my age, or imply you are a liar) *inadvertently* if, in the course of executing by the use of some medium of communication some other act A_2 (say, reminiscing about my war service), I fail to exercise such meticulous supervision over the choice and arrangement of the signs as would have been needed to ensure that. . . . It is interesting to note how such adverbs lead parallel lives, one in connection with physical actions ("doing") and the other in connection with acts of communication ("saying"), or sometimes also in connection with acts of "thinking" ("inadvertently assumed").

with *un-* or *in-*, those in another with *-less* ("aimless," "reckless," "heed-
less," etc.), and those in another with *mis-* ("mistake," "misconception,"
"misjudgment," etc.)? Why care*less*ly but *in*attentively? Perhaps care
and attention, so often linked, are rather different. Here are remunera-
tive exercises.

4. *The machinery of action.* Not merely do adverbial expressions pick
out classes of actions, they also pick out the internal detail of the machinery of doing actions, or the departments into which the business of
doing actions is organized. There is for example the stage at which
we have actually to *carry out* some action upon which we embark—
perhaps we have to make certain bodily movements or to make a speech.
In the course of actually *doing* these things (getting weaving) we have
to pay (some) attention to what we are doing and to take (some)
care to guard against (likely) dangers: we may need to use judgment or
tact: we must exercise sufficient control over our bodily parts: and so
on. Inattention, carelessness, errors of judgment, tactlessness, clumsi-·
ness, all these and others are ills (with attendant excuses) which affect
one specific stage in the machinery of action, the *executive* stage, the
stage where we *muff* it. But there are many other departments in the
business too, each of which is to be traced and mapped through its cluster
of appropriate verbs and adverbs. Obviously there are departments of
intelligence and planning, of decision and resolve, and so on: but I shall
mention one in particular, too often overlooked, where troubles and
excuses abound. It happens to us, in military life, to be in receipt of
excellent intelligence, to be also in self-conscious possession of excellent
principles (the five golden rules for winning victories), and yet to hit
upon a plan of action which leads to disaster. One way in which this
can happen is through failure at the stage of *appreciation* of the situation, that is at the stage where we are required to cast our excellent
intelligence into such a form, under such heads and with such weights
attached, that our equally excellent principles can be brought to bear
on it properly, in a way to yield the right answer.[10] So too in real, or
rather civilian, life, in moral or practical affairs, we can know the
facts and yet look at them mistakenly or perversely, or not fully realize
or appreciate something, or even be under a total misconception. Many
expressions of excuse indicate failure at this particularly tricky stage:
even thoughtlessness, inconsiderateness, lack of imagination, are perhaps
less matters of failure in intelligence or planning than might be supposed, and more matters of failure to appreciate the situation. A course
of E. M. Forster and we see things differently: yet perhaps we know
no more and are no cleverer.

---

[10] We know all about how to do quadratics: we know all the needful facts
about pipes, cisterns, hours and plumbers: yet we reach the answer "3¾ men."
We have failed to cast our facts correctly into mathematical form.

5. *Standards of the unacceptable.* It is characteristic of excuses to be "unacceptable": given, I suppose, almost any excuse, there will be cases of such a kind or of such gravity that "we will not accept" it. It is interesting to detect the standards and codes we thus invoke. The extent of the supervision we exercise over the execution of any act can never be quite unlimited, and usually is expected to fall within fairly definite limits ("due care and attention") in the case of acts of some general kind, though of course we set very different limits in different cases. We may plead that we trod on the snail inadvertently: but not on a baby —you ought to look where you are putting your great feet. Of course it *was* (*really*), if you like, inadvertence: but that word constitutes a plea, which is not going to be allowed, because of standards. And if you try it on, you will be subscribing to such dreadful standards that your last state will be worse than your first. Or again, we set different standards, and will accept different excuses, in the case of acts which are rule-governed, like spelling, and which we are expected absolutely to get right, from those we set and accept for less stereotyped actions: a wrong spelling may be a slip, but hardly an accident, a winged beater may be an accident, but hardly a slip.

6. *Combination, dissociation, and complication.* A belief in opposites and dichotomies encourages, among other things, a blindness to the combinations and dissociations of adverbs that are possible, even to such obvious facts as that we can act at once on impulse and intentionally, or that we can do an action intentionally yet for all that not deliberately, still less on purpose. We walk along the cliff, and I feel a sudden impulse to push you over, which I promptly do: I acted on impulse, yet I certainly intended to push you over, and may even have devised a little ruse to achieve it: yet even then I did not act deliberately, for I did not (stop to) ask myself whether to do it or not.

It is worth bearing in mind, too, the general rule that we must not expect to find simple labels for complicated cases. If a mistake results in an accident, it will not do to ask whether "it" was an accident or a mistake, or to demand some briefer description of "it." Here the natural economy of language operates: if the words already available for simple cases suffice in combination to describe a complicated case, there will be need for special reasons before a special new word is invented for the complication. Besides, however well-equipped our language, it can never be forearmed against all possible cases that may arise and call for description: fact is richer than diction.

7. *Regina* v. *Finney.* Often the complexity and difficulty of a case is considerable. I will quote the case of *Regina* v. *Finney*:[11]

---

[11] A somewhat distressing favorite in the class that Hart used to conduct with me in the years soon after the war. The italics are mine.

Shrewsbury Assizes.   1874.   12 Cox 625.
Prisoner was indicted for the manslaughter of Thomas Watkins.
The Prisoner was an attendant at a lunatic asylum. Being in
charge of a lunatic, who was bathing, he turned on hot water into
the bath, and thereby scalded him to death. The facts appeared to
be truly set forth in the statement of the prisoner made before the
committing magistrate, as follows: "I had bathed Watkins, and
had loosed the bath out. *I intended putting in a clean bath,* and
asked Watkins if he would get out. At this time *my attention was
drawn* to the next bath by the new attendant, who was asking me
a question; and *my attention was taken from the bath* where Watkins was. I put my hand down to turn water on in the bath where
Thomas Watkins was. *I did not intend to turn the hot water,* and
I made a mistake in the tap. I did not know what I had done until
I heard Thomas Watkins shout out; and *I did not find my mistake
out till* I saw the steam from the water. You cannot get water in
this bath when they are drawing water at the other bath; but at
other times it shoots out like a water gun when the other baths are
not in use. . . ."
(It was proved that the lunatic had such possession of his facul-
ties as would enable him to understand what was said to him, and
to get out of the bath.)
A. Young (for Prisoner). The death *resulted from accident.*
There was no such *culpable negligence* on the part of the prisoner
as will support this indictment. A *culpable mistake,* or some degree
of *culpable negligence,* causing death, will not support a charge of
manslaughter; unless the *negligence* be so gross as to be *reckless.*
(*R. v. Noakes.*)
Lush, J. To render a person liable for *neglect of duty* there must
be such a degree of culpability as to amount to *gross negligence* on
his part. If you accept the prisoner's own statement, you find no
such amount of *negligence* as would come within this definition.
It is not every little *trip or mistake* that will make a man so liable.
It was the duty of the attendant not to let hot water into the bath
while the patient was therein. According to the prisoner's own
account, *he did not believe that* he was letting the hot water in
while the deceased remained there. The lunatic was, we have heard,
a man capable of getting out by himself and of understanding what
was said to him. He was told to get out. A new attendant who had
come on this day, was at an adjoining bath and he *took off the
prisoner's attention.* Now, if the prisoner, knowing that the man
was in the bath, had turned on the tap, and turned on the hot water, instead of the cold water, I should have said there was gross negligence; for he ought to have looked to see. But from his own account
he had told the deceased to get out, and *thought he had got out.*
If you think that indicates gross *carelessness,* then you should find
the prisoner guilty of manslaughter. But if you think it *inadvertence*

not amounting to culpability—i.e., what is properly termed an *accident*—then the prisoner is not liable.

Verdict, Not guilty.

In this case there are two morals that I will point. (1) Both counsel and judge make very free use of a large number of terms of excuse, using several as though they were, and even stating them to be, indifferent or equivalent when they are not, and presenting as alternatives those that are not. (2) It is constantly difficult to be sure *what* act it is that counsel or judge is suggesting might be qualified by what expression of excuse. The learned judge's concluding direction is a paradigm of these faults.[12] Finney, by contrast, stands out as an evident master of the Queen's English. He is explicit as to each of his acts and states, mental and physical: he uses different, and the correct, adverbs in connection with each: and he makes no attempt to boil down.

8. *Small distinctions, and big too.* It should go without saying that terms of excuse are not equivalent, and that it matters which we use: we need to distinguish inadvertence not merely from (save the mark) such things as mistake and accident, but from such nearer neighbors as, say, aberration and absence of mind. By imagining cases with vividness and fullness we should be able to decide in which precise terms to describe, say, Miss Plimsoll's action in writing, so carefully, "DAIRY" on her fine new book: we should be able to distinguish between sheer, mere, pure, and simple mistake or inadvertence. Yet unfortunately, at least when in the grip of thought, we fail not merely at these stiffer hurdles. We equate even—I have seen it done—"inadvertently" with "automatically": as though to say I trod on your toe inadvertently means to say I trod on it automatically. Or we collapse succumbing to temptation into losing control of ourselves—a bad patch, this, for telescoping.[13]

---

[12] Not but what he probably manages to convey his meaning somehow or other. Judges seem to acquire a knack of conveying meaning, and even carrying conviction, through the use of a pithy Anglo-Saxon which sometimes has literally no meaning at all. Wishing to distinguish the case of shooting at a post in the belief that it was an enemy, as *not* an "attempt," from the case of picking an empty pocket in the belief that money was in it, which *is* an "attempt," the judge explains that in shooting at the post "the man is never on the thing at all."

[13] Plato, I suppose, and after him Aristotle, fastened this confusion upon us, as bad in its day and way as the later, grotesque, confusion of moral weakness with weakness of will. I am very partial to ice cream, and a bombe is served divided into segments corresponding one to one with the persons at High Table: I am tempted to help myself to two segments and do so, thus succumbing to temptation and even conceivably (but why necessarily?) going against my principles. But do I lose control of myself? Do I raven, do I snatch the morsels from the dish and wolf them down, impervious to the consternation of my colleagues? Not a bit of it. We often succumb to temptation with calm and even with finesse.

All this is not so much a *lesson* from the study of excuses as the very object of it.

9. *The exact phrase and its place in the sentence.* It is not enough, either, to attend simply to the "key" word: notice must also be taken of the full and exact form of the expression used. In considering mistakes, we have to consider seriatim "by mistake," "owing to a mistake," "mistakenly," "it was a mistake to," "to make a mistake in or over or about," "to be mistaken about," and so on: in considering purpose, we have to consider "on," "with the," "for the," etc., besides "purposeful," "purposeless," and the like. These varying expressions may function quite differently—and usually do, or why should we burden ourselves with more than one of them?

Care must be taken too to observe the precise position of an adverbial expression in the sentence. This should of course indicate what verb it is being used to modify: but more than that, the position can also affect the *sense* of the expression, i.e., the way in which it modifies that verb. Compare, for example:

> a_1 He clumsily trod on the snail.
> a_2 Clumsily he trod on the snail.
> b_1 He trod clumsily on the snail.
> b_2 He trod on the snail clumsily.

Here, in a_1 and a_2 we describe his treading on the creature at all as a piece of clumsiness, incidental, we imply, to his performance of some other action: but with b_1 and b_2 to tread on it is, very likely, his aim or policy, what we criticize is his execution of the feat.[14] Many adverbs, though far from all (not, for example, "purposely") are used in these two typically different ways.

10. *The style of performance.* With some adverbs the distinction between the two senses referred to in the last paragraph is carried a stage further. "He ate his soup deliberately" may mean, like "He deliberately ate his soup," that his eating his soup was a deliberate act, one perhaps that he thought would annoy somebody, as it would more commonly if he deliberately ate *my* soup, and which he decided to do: but it will often mean that he went through the performance of eating his soup in a noteworthy manner or *style*—pause after each mouthful, careful choice of point of entry for the spoon, sucking of moustaches, and so on. That is, it will mean that he ate *with* deliberation rather than *after* deliberation. The style of the performance, slow and unhurried, is understandably called "deliberate" because each movement *has the typi-*

---

[14] As a matter of fact, most of these examples *can* be understood the other way, especially if we allow ourselves inflections of the voice, or commas, or contexts. a_2 might be a poetic inversion for b_2: b_1, perhaps with commas round the "clumsily," might be used for a_1: and so on. Still, the two senses are clearly enough distinguishable.

cal look of a deliberate act: but it is scarcely being said that the making of each motion *is* a deliberate act or that he is "literally" deliberating. This case, then, is more extreme than that of "clumsily," which does in both uses describe literally a manner of performing.

It is worth watching out for this secondary use when scrutinizing any particular adverbial expression: when it definitely does not exist, the reason is worth inquiring into. Sometimes it is very hard to be sure whether it does exist or does not: it does, one would think, with "carelessly," it does not with "inadvertently," but does it or does it not with "absent-mindedly" or "aimlessly"? In some cases a word akin to but distinct from the primary adverb is used for this special role of describing a style of performance: we use "purposefully" in this way, but never "purposely."

11. *What modifies what?* The judge in *Regina* v. *Finney* does not make clear what event is being excused in what way. "If you think that indicates gross carelessness, then. . . . But if you think it inadvertence not amounting to culpability—i.e., what is properly called an accident— then. . . ." Apparently he means that Finney may have *turned on the hot tap* inadvertently:[15] does he mean also that the tap may have been turned accidentally, or rather that *Watkins may have been scalded* and killed accidentally? And was the carelessness in turning the tap or in thinking Watkins had got out? Many disputes as to what excuse we should properly use arise because we will not trouble to state explicitly *what* is being excused.

To do so is all the more vital because it is in principle always open to us, along various lines, to describe or refer to "what I did" in so many different ways. This is altogether too large a theme to elaborate here. Apart from the more general and obvious problems of the use of "tendentious" descriptive terms, there are many special problems in the particular case of "actions." Should we say, are we saying, that he took her money, or that he robbed her? That he knocked a ball into a hole, or that he sank a putt? That he said "Done," or that he accepted an offer? How far, that is, are motives, intentions, and conventions to be part of the description of actions? And more especially here, what is *an* or *one* or *the* action? For we can generally split up what might be

---

[15] What Finney says is different: he says he "made a mistake in the tap." This is the basic use of "mistake," where we simply, and not necessarily accountably, take the wrong one. Finney here attempts to account for his mistake, by saying that his attention was distracted. But suppose the order is "Right turn" and I turn left: no doubt the sergeant will insinuate that my attention was distracted, or that I cannot distinguish my right from my left—but it was not and I can; this was a simple, pure mistake. As often happens. Neither I nor the sergeant will suggest that there was any accident, or any inadvertence either. If Finney had turned the hot tap inadvertently, then it would have been knocked, say, in reaching for the cold tap: a different story.

named as one action in several distinct ways, into different *stretches* or
phases or *stages*. Stages have already been mentioned: we can dismantle
the machinery of the act, and describe (and excuse) separately the intelligence, the appreciation, the planning, the decision, the execution, and
so forth. Phases are rather different: we can say that he painted a picture
or fought a campaign, or else we can say that first he laid on this stroke
of paint and then that, first he fought this action and then that.
Stretches are different again: a single term descriptive of what he did
may be made to cover either a smaller or a larger stretch of events,
those excluded by the narrower description being then called "consequences" or "results" or "effects" or the like of his act. So here we can
describe Finney's act *either* as turning on the hot tap, which he did by
mistake, with the result that Watkins was scalded, *or* as scalding Watkins, which he did *not* do by mistake.

It is very evident that the problems of excuses and tnose of the different descriptions of actions are throughout bound up with each other.

12. *Trailing clouds of etymology*. It is these considerations that bring
us up so forcibly against some of the most difficult words in the whole
story of Excuses, such words as "result," "effect," and "consequence,"
or again as "intention," "purpose," and "motive." I will mention two
points of method which are, experience has convinced me, indispensable
aids at these levels.

One is that a word never—well, hardly ever—shakes off its etymology
and its formation. In spite of all changes in and extensions of and additions to its meanings, and indeed rather pervading and governing these,
there will still persist the old idea. In an *accident* something befalls: by
mistake you take the wrong one: in *error* you stray: when you act
deliberately you act after weighing it up (*not* after thinking out ways
and means). It is worth asking ourselves whether we know the etymology of "result" or of "spontaneously," and worth remembering that
"unwillingly" and "involuntarily" come from very different sources.

And the second point is connected with this. Going back into the
history of a word, very often into Latin, we come back pretty commonly to pictures or *models* of how things happen or are done. These
models may be fairly sophisticated and recent, as is perhaps the case with
"motive" or "impulse," but one of the commonest and most primitive
types of model is one which is apt to baffle us through its very natural-
ness and simplicity. We take *some very simple action*, like shoving a
stone, usually as done by and viewed by oneself, and use *this*, with the
features distinguishable in it, as our model in terms of which to talk
about other actions and events: and we continue to do so, scarcely realiz-
ing it, even when these other actions are pretty remote and perhaps
much more interesting to us in their own right than the acts originally
used in constructing the model ever were, and even when the model is

really distorting the facts rather than helping us to observe them. In primitive cases we may get to see clearly the differences between, say, "results," "effects," and "consequences," and yet discover that these differences are no longer clear, and the terms themselves no longer of real service to us, in the more complicated cases where we had been bandying them about most freely. A model must be recognized for what it is. "Causing," I suppose, was a notion taken from a man's own experience of doing simple actions, and by primitive man every event was construed in terms of this model: every event has a cause, that is, every event is an action done by somebody—if not by a man, then by a quasiman, a spirit. When, later, events which are *not* actions are realized to be such, we still say that they must be "caused," and the word snares us: we are struggling to ascribe to it a new, unanthropomorphic meaning, yet constantly, in searching for its analysis, we unearth and incorporate the lineaments of the ancient model. As happened even to Hume, and consequently to Kant. Examining such a word historically, we may well find that it has been extended to cases that have by now too tenuous a relation to the model case, that it is a source of confusion and superstition.

There is too another danger in words that invoke models, half-forgotten or not. It must be remembered that there is no necessity whatsoever that the various models used in creating our vocabulary, primitive or recent, should all fit together neatly as parts into one single, total model or scheme of, for instance, the doing of actions. It is possible, and indeed highly likely, that our assortment of models will include some, or many, that are overlapping, conflicting, or more generally simply *disparate*.[16]

13. In spite of the wide and acute observation of the phenomena of action embodied in ordinary speech, modern scientists have been able, it seems to me, to reveal its inadequacy at numerous points, if only because they have had access to more comprehensive data and have studied them with more catholic and dispassionate interest than the ordinary

---

[16] This is by way of a general warning in philosophy. It seems to be too readily assumed that if we can only discover the true meanings of each of a cluster of key terms, usually historic terms, that we use in some particular field (as, for example, "right," "good," and the rest in morals), then it must without question transpire that each will fit into place in some single, interlocking, consistent, conceptual scheme. Not only is there no reason to assume this, but all historical probability is against it, especially in the case of a language derived from such various civilizations as ours is. We may cheerfully use, and with weight, terms which are not so much head-on incompatible as simply disparate, which just do not fit in or even on. Just as we cheerfully subscribe to, or have the grace to be torn between, simply disparate ideals—why *must* there be a conceivable amalgam, the Good Life for Man?

man, or even the lawyer, has had occasion to do. I will conclude with two examples.

Observation of animal behavior shows that regularly, when an animal is embarked on some recognizable pattern of behavior but meets in the course of it with an insuperable obstacle, it will betake itself to energetic, but quite unrelated, activity of some wild kind, such as standing on its head. This phenomenon is called "displacement behavior" and is well identifiable. If now, in the light of this, we look back at ordinary human life, we see that displacement behavior bulks quite large in it: yet we have apparently no word, or at least no clear and simple word, for it. If, when thwarted, we stand on our heads or wiggle our toes, then we are not exactly *just* standing on our heads, don't you know, in the ordinary way, yet is there any convenient adverbial expression we can insert to do the trick? "In desperation"?

Take, again, "compulsive" behavior, however exactly psychologists define it, compulsive washing for example. There are of course hints in ordinary speech that we do things in this way—"just feel I have to," "shouldn't feel comfortable unless I did," and the like: but there is no adverbial expression satisfactorily pre-empted for it, as "compulsively" is. This is understandable enough, since compulsive behavior, like displacement behavior, is not in general going to be of great practical importance.

Here I leave and commend the subject to you.

ON THE VERIFICATION

OF STATEMENTS

ABOUT ORDINARY LANGUAGE[1]

BENSON MATES

In this paper I shall discuss certain difficulties which seem to me to stand in the way of understanding or properly appreciating the work of the so-called ordinary language philosophers. These difficulties concern the interpretation of the various seemingly factual statements which such philosophers make about language. I am mainly interested in the question of how one would go about verifying these statements; insofar as meaning is bound up with verification, this is also a question of their meaning. Of course, it is possible to pretend that no clarification is required at all, that the sense of assertions about the ordinary use of language is perfectly obvious, or at least sufficiently so for the purposes at hand. But I do not think that such optimism is justified. Even among those who can claim to be "in the know" or to "get the point" there are wide disagreements both as to the truth and as to the meaning of given

From Inquiry, *Vol. I (1958). Reprinted by permission of the author and the editor of* Inquiry.
[1] This paper and the one which succeeds it, by Professor Cavell, were read as parts of a symposium at a meeting of the American Philosophical Association, Pacific Coast Division, on December 19, 1957.

assertions of the sort under consideration, and these disagreements are by themselves a basis for skepticism. When in addition it is seen that such assertions play a crucial role in the discussions which are supposed to answer, dissolve, or somehow get rid of the traditional problems of philosophy, a philosopher may perhaps be excused for looking at the matter a little more closely.

First, a parenthetical remark about terminology. As is always the case when one attempts to formulate objections to a philosophical position of scope and subtlety, there is here the problem of finding a convenient vocabulary which does not beg too many questions. I shall make use of such terms as "analytic," "synthetic," "meaning," "sense," "denotation," in the hope that I am not thereby drawing a number of red herring across the trail, and in the belief that if necessary I could reformulate my points without the use of these terms, though with a considerable loss of compactness. For instance, when I ask whether a given statement about ordinary language is normative or descriptive, and whether it is analytic or synthetic, I am not asking questions to which the alleged difficulties with the fringes of these terms are decisively relevant. Instead, I merely wish to know with what attitude the given statement is to be confronted; for instance, is it to be regarded as a recommendation, so that an appropriate query is "What will be gained by following this advice?" or is it to be regarded as true or false? And if it is to be taken as true or false, does the author intend it as true by virtue of the meanings of the terms involved, or does he consider himself to have made a statement the truth-value of which depends upon matters of fact? The answers to such questions will fundamentally affect our understanding of the given statement, and they do not, so far as I can see, need to involve us in any of the philosophical tangles which are supposed to be connected with the terms "normative" and "analytic." I believe that somewhat analogous comments apply to the other cases in which I make use of notorious philosophical terminology.

It will be useful to have before us some examples of the type of statement under consideration. Accordingly I quote a passage from Professor Gilbert Ryle's treatment of the Freedom of the Will:

> It should be noticed that while ordinary folk, magistrates, parents and teachers, generally apply the words "voluntary" and "involuntary" to actions in one way, philosophers often apply them in quite another way.
>
> In their most ordinary employment "voluntary" and "involuntary" are used, with a few minor elasticities, as adjectives applying to actions which ought not to be done. We discuss whether someone's action was voluntary or not only when the action seems to have been his fault. . . . In the same way in ordinary life we raise questions of responsibility only when someone is charged, justly or

unjustly, with an offence. It makes sense, in this use, to ask whether
a boy was responsible for breaking a window, but not whether he
was responsible for finishing his homework in good time. . . .

   In this ordinary use, then, it is absurd to discuss whether satisfac-
tory, correct or admirable performances are voluntary or involuntary. . . .

   But philosophers, in discussing what constitutes acts voluntary or
involuntary, tend to describe as voluntary not only reprehensible
but also meritorious actions, not only things that are someone's
fault but also things that are to his credit. The motives underlying
their unwitting extension of the ordinary sense of "voluntary"
. . . will be considered later. . . .

   The tangle of largely spurious problems, known as the problem
of the Freedom of the Will, partly derives from this unconsciously
stretched use of "voluntary." . . .[2]

These, then, are examples of the sort of remark I wish to consider.
They may not be the best examples that could have been chosen, but
they do have the not inconsiderable merit of being relatively lucid. Professor Ryle seems here to assert that the ordinary use of the word "voluntary" is quite different from the philosophic use. He does not mean
merely that the ordinary man seldom talks philosophy. The difference
between the ordinary use and the philosophic use hinges rather upon the
alleged fact that the ordinary man applies the word "voluntary" almost
exclusively to actions which ought not to be done, while the philosopher
stretches it to cover meritorious actions as well. Now although the
question whether Professor Ryle is right or wrong in this particular case
is not essential to the point of the present paper, I will say at once (1)
that I very much doubt whether as a matter of fact the ordinary man
does apply the term "voluntary" only to actions which (he thinks)
ought not to be done, and (2) that even if this were shown to be the
case, it would not have decisive relevance to a determination of the
ordinary use of the word "voluntary." Some other factor, such as perhaps a disposition on the part of the ordinary man to talk more about
things of which he disapproves than about things of which he approves,
could by itself account for a relatively frequent application of the word
"voluntary" to disapproved actions, even if the word were simply being
used in one of its dictionary senses, e.g., "proceeding from the will or
from one's own choice or full consent." In short, at first glance it seems
that Professor Ryle's assertion about the ordinary use of the word "voluntary" is false, and, moreover, that it is based upon doubtful evidence
which would be entirely insufficient even if it were sound.

   When one comes to so drastic a conclusion about an assertion seriously

---

[2] Gilbert Ryle, *The Concept of Mind* (London: Hutchinson and Co., Ltd.,
1949), pp. 69ff.

made, it is time to reconsider the possibility that one has not understood what was asserted. For further light we may consult an article entitled "Ordinary Language," [3] in which Professor Ryle attempts by means of a distinction between use and usage to indicate why empirical studies like those of the lexicographers or philologists are irrelevant to the truth of statements about the ordinary use of language. Such studies have a place in determining the *usage* of a word, he says, but not in determining the *use*. Uses are ways or techniques of doing the thing, the more or less widely prevailing practice of doing which constitutes the usage. He explains further that "ordinary use" is to be contrasted with "non-stock use," and that in general "use" contrasts in these contexts with "misuse." Now it seems to me that Professor Ryle fails to make good the alleged distinction between use and usage, and still less the point that through confusion in this matter philosophers have misunderstood the character of claims that the ordinary use of a word is this or that. Nevertheless, his discussion is not without significance for the matters we are considering: it appears to indicate that for him there is some sort of normative element in assertions about ordinary use. If the opposite of use is misuse, then use must be somehow right, proper, or correct. It is not easy to see how this can be applied to statements like those quoted about the word "voluntary," but perhaps Professor Ryle's discussion in that passage comes down to an assertion that to predicate the word "voluntary" of praiseworthy actions is to misuse the word, presumably in some sense of "misuse" which cannot be defined statistically. But if this is the way the wind blows, it would be instructive to have an indication of the standards or goals with reference to which the term "misuse" is applicable. What authority deems it wrong to use the word "voluntary" as the philosopher does? What unwelcome consequences would attend the proscribed use? Surely the point is not merely that if you use the word "voluntary" just as the philosopher does, you may find yourself entangled in the philosophic problem of the Freedom of the Will.

Despite Professor Ryle's own explanations, I am reluctant to believe that the expression "ordinary use" is really a normative term for the ordinary language philosophers. The way in which they use it seems better explained on the hypothesis that it is a rough descriptive term, employed with little definiteness of intention, and that there is in addition a *belief,* not part of the meaning of "ordinary use," to the effect that it is somehow wrong or inadvisable, or at least dangerous, to use ordinary words in ways different from those in which the ordinary man uses them. It is further supposed, and often expressly asserted, that in daily life words function well enough and lead to no great problems. In

---

[3] Ryle, "Ordinary Language." (See above, pp. 24ff.)

any case, although all forms of "nose-counting" are deprecated in these quarters, it often happens that when support is offered for an assertion that the ordinary use of a given word is thus and so, this support takes the form of an attempt to remind or convince us that the use in question is indeed quite frequent among "ordinary folk, magistrates, parents and teachers." In other words, the statement is taken as having a factual basis and presumably as refutable by observation of the ordinary folk, magistrates, parents and teachers.

This brings me to the question of how one might verify a statement about the ordinary use of a word or phrase, when the statement is interpreted neither as a piece of advice nor as a claim that the use is sanctioned by authority. It is necessary here to make passing mention of a point of view, or rather a dodge, which cannot be taken very seriously. This is the comfortable suggestion that the average adult has already amassed such a tremendous amount of empirical information about the use of his native language, that he can depend upon his own intuition or memory and need not undertake a laborious questioning of other people, even when he is dealing with the tricky terms which are central in philosophical problems. Such an assertion is itself an empirical hypothesis, of a sort which used to be invoked in favor of armchair psychology, and it is not borne out by the facts.[4] It has been found that even relatively careful authors are often not reliable reporters of their *own* linguistic behavior, let alone that of others. (Indeed, this is hardly surprising in view of the fact that most of the time we use language in a more or less automatic manner.) The weakness of the hypothesis is further revealed by the fact that the intuitive findings of different people, even of different experts, are often inconsistent. Thus, for example, while Professor Ryle tells us that "voluntary" and "involuntary" in their ordinary use are applied only to actions which ought not to be done, his colleague Professor Austin states in another connection: ". . . for example, take 'voluntarily' and 'involuntarily': we may join the army or make a gift voluntarily, we may hiccough or make a small gesture involuntarily . . ."[5] If agreement about usage cannot be reached within so restricted a sample as the class of Oxford Professors of Philosophy, what are the prospects when the sample is enlarged?

Let us now look at the question of how to verify an assertion that a

---

[4] I do not deny that the armchair method is adequate for many purposes. Perhaps it is adequate even for deciding the correctness or incorrectness of statements like those of Professor Ryle about "voluntary." I would not trust it, however, to decide such a question as whether the ordinary use of "inadvertently" is the same as that of "automatically" (as applied to actions). [Cf. J. L. Austin, "A Plea for Excuses." (See above, p. 58.)] Of course, even in these cases I do not propose to dispense with it, but only to add to it.

[5] *Ibid.*, p. 53.

given person uses a word in a given way or with a given sense. It seems to me that, roughly speaking, there are two basic approaches, which I shall call the "extensional" and the "intensional," though any really adequate procedure will probably have to be a combination of both. In the extensional approach one observes a reasonably large class of cases in which the subject applies the word, and then one "sees" or "elicits" the meaning by finding what is common to these cases. For some reason or other this method, with all of its obvious difficulties, is thought by many people to be more scientific than the intensional approach. In the latter, one asks the subject what he means by the given word or how he uses it; the one proceeds in Socratic fashion to test this first answer by confronting the subject with counterexamples and borderline cases, and so on until the subject settles down more or less permanently upon a definition or account. The difficulties with this method are also very considerable, and I hold no particular brief for it. I only wish to say that it has just as legitimate a claim to be "right" as the extensional method has. Things become interesting when, as will often happen, the two approaches give different results. What the analyst sees in common among the cases to which the subject applies the term may have little or nothing to do with what the subject says he means by the term; and, further, the subject may in fact apply the term to cases which lack the characteristics which he himself considers essential for proper application of the term. In whatever manner these conflicts are to be resolved, I wish only to repeat that the outcome of the intensional approach is as much a characterization of ordinary usage as the outcome of the extensional approach, assuming of course that the same subjects are involved. Thus, even if Professor Ryle had determined that ordinary folk in fact apply the word "voluntary" only to actions which ought not to be done, while philosophers apply it to meritorious actions as well, he would be far from establishing that philosophers and ordinary folk apply the word "voluntary" in different ways, i.e., attach different senses to it.[6] For if he had proceeded by the intensional route he might have found that both philosophers and ordinary folk tend to give the same sort of definition or account—perhaps something similar to what one finds in the dictionary—and this would have been evidence that they use the term in the *same* sense. Both approaches may lead to interesting results, but I do not see that one is scientific and the other is not, or that one is useful and the other is not.

Now the ordinary language philosophers, I believe, tend toward an armchair version of the extensional method, though sometimes they read the dictionary for intensional guidance before surveying the cases in which they know or suppose the term would be applied. This exten-

---

[6] Note Ryle's use of the word "sense" in the passage quoted.

sional approach appears in the quoted passage from Professor Ryle,[7] and it may also be seen in the following quotation from J. O. Urmson's article, "Some Questions Concerning Validity":

> In his popular book, *The Nature of the Physical World,* . . . Eddington said in effect that desks were not really solid. Miss Stebbing, in her book *Philosophy and the Physicists* [showed] that this way of putting things involved illegitimate mystification; this she did by simply pointing out that if one asked what we ordinarily mean by *solid* we immediately realise that we mean something like "of the consistency of such things as desks." Thus she showed conclusively that the novelty of scientific theory does not consist, as had been unfortunately suggested, in showing the inappropriateness of ordinary descriptive language.[8]

I interpret (perhaps erroneously) Urmson and Stebbing to be saying that if you look and see to which objects people regularly apply the word "solid," you will find that by and large these objects have the consistency of such things as desks. But from this it does not follow that by "solid" we *mean* something like "of the consistency of such things as desks." If you want to know what we mean by "solid," you should in addition ask us; the answers will very likely be inconclusive, but they will be relevant. Perhaps they will tend to converge on several senses, one of which could be "not hollow, having its interior entirely filled with matter." If you follow out *this* strand of the ordinary use of "solid" it will no longer appear so obvious that Eddington was using "solid" in a new or mystifying sense when he said that desks are not really solid. Indeed, the effectiveness of Eddington's remark seems to derive from the fact that the properties which one is inclined to regard as the defining properties of solidity do not really belong to the objects to which we customarily apply the term "solid," and the interest of this fact is in no way diminished by repeating "Oh, but we *do* apply the word 'solid' to such things as desks." Of course we do, but we also say that by "solid" we mean "having its interior entirely filled with matter," or something like that. The collision is *within* ordinary usage, and not between it and scientific theory.

I should like now to mention some of the difficulties which attend the two methods I have discussed. Only when one gets down to cases do these problems appear with clarity, and in this general account I can list just a few. In connection with the extensional approach we have the problem of deciding which occurrences of the word are to be con-

---

[7] I.e., he tries to show that the philosophic sense is different from the ordinary sense, using as evidence information that the philosophic extension is different from the ordinary extension.

[8] J. O. Urmson, "Some Questions Concerning Validity," *Revue internationale de philosophie,* Vol. VII (1953), 217ff.; reprinted in *Essays in Conceptual Analysis,* Antony Flew, ed. (London: Macmillan & Co., Ltd., 1956).

sidered (especially when the word is thought to have different senses) and what are the relevant features of the objects to which the word is applied or of the situations in which it is applied. Much depends upon how these objects or situations are described (or "thought of") in the data from which the meaning is to be "elicited." [9] Further, shall we describe the objects and situations in terms of the properties which they really have, or in terms of the properties which they are thought by the subject to have? (If the latter alternative is chosen, then even the extensional approach might lead to the conclusion that tables are not really solid, in the ordinary sense of "solid.") When it comes to seeing what is common to the various items which make up the extension, the difficulties become still worse. The objects in any collection will have infinitely many properties in common; furthermore, two words with quite different senses may happen to have the same extension or, even more likely, their extensions may happen to coincide in the domain investigated. Thus perhaps Professor Ryle happened to consider only some part of the extension of "voluntary act" which is also a part of the extension of "voluntary act that ought not to be done." On top of all these problems is the problem of determining what will justify the conclusion that a word has more than one sense or use. We shall never find a case in which it is not true that all items of the extension have *something* in common, even when on other grounds we are inclined to say that the word in question has two senses. Some principle is needed for singling out the "real" or "important" properties, but it is not easy to state what that would be. In view of all these matters it becomes apparent that the task of looking at the applications of a word and "seeing" what it means is not so simple, after all.

Before describing some of the difficulties attending the intensional approach I should like to add one more observation which pertains mainly to the extensional approach. We have all heard the wearying platitude that "you can't separate" the meaning of a word from the entire context in which it occurs, including not only the actual linguistic context but also the aims, feelings, beliefs, and hopes of the speaker, the same for the listener and any bystanders, the social situation, the physical surroundings, the historical background, the rules of the game, and so on ad infinitum. There is no doubt some truth in this, but I fail to see how it helps one get started in an empirical investigation of language. At the very least, provisional divisions of the subject have to be made somewhere. It seems to me that there is much to be said for the well-known syntax-semantics-pragmatics division, and that often many of the factors which the ordinary language philosophers find in

---

[9] E.g., in Ryle's case they could be described or taken as actions which ought not to be done, or as actions proceeding from the will or from the individual's own choice or full consent, or in any of a number of other ways.

common among the cases in which an expression is employed belong
more to the pragmatics of the expression than to its semantics. In particular, most of the facts which are expressed by statements of the form
"He wouldn't say that unless he . . ." belong in the category of the
pragmatics of the expression and should be avoided when "eliciting"
or "seeing" the meaning. To take an example, consider all the fuss about
the sentence "I know it, but I may be wrong," which has been called
everything from "contradiction" to "nonsense." Perhaps it is true that
ordinarily I wouldn't say "I know it" unless I felt great confidence in
what I was asserting, and it might also be true that ordinarily I
wouldn't say "I may be wrong" unless I felt only a small amount of
such confidence. So that if I say "I know it, but I may be wrong" the
listener may be momentarily befuddled before he hits upon the right
diagnosis of the form "He wouldn't say that unless he. . . ." But all
this does not suffice to show that "I know it, but I may be wrong" is
contradictory or nonsensical according to ordinary usage. The confidence
I signify by saying "I know it" does not have to be mentioned in giving
a semantical account of the word "know," but only in describing its
pragmatics. Likewise, when I say "I may be wrong" I do not *imply*
that I have no confidence in what I have previously asserted; I only
indicate it. If I do have the confidence and yet say "I may be wrong,"
I have not told a falsehood, though I may indeed have misled someone.
Limitation of time prevents my going further into this matter, and
I only bring it up so as to be able to formulate the following: it seems
to me that not only do the ordinary language philosophers tend toward
an armchair version of the extensional method, but also they are inclined
to overlook the semantic-pragmatic distinction when they find what is
common to the situations in which a given word is used. If, in the
example concerning "voluntary," Professor Ryle means that the ordinary
man applies the word only to actions of which he disapproves, while the
philosopher applies it to approved actions as well, and that hence the
philosopher uses the word in a stretched, extraordinary sense, then this
would be an example of the sort of semantic-pragmatic confusion which
I am here trying to describe.[10]

---

[10] Consider the sentence, "Jones disapproves of playing golf on Sunday." In
this sentence the word "Jones" occurs directly, while the expression "playing
golf on Sunday" occurs obliquely. Thus, the truth-value of the given sentence
may be reversed when the expression "playing golf on Sunday" is replaced by
an expression having the same denotation but different sense. Now since I use
the word "property" in such a way as to satisfy Leibniz' Law (in the form: if
A is the same as B, then any property of A is a property of B), I regard the
given sentence as expressing a property of Jones but not as expressing a property of the act of playing golf on Sunday. Consequently I am led to hold that
although the properties of an act will in general be relevant to the semantics
of any expression referring to that act, the approval or disapproval of an act
by someone does not constitute one of its properties.

The intensional approach to the problem of verifying assertions about meaning or use seems to involve us in a conceptual difficulty of its own. If we are to do justice to the notions (1) that what an individual means by a word depends at least in part upon what he *wants* to mean by that word, and (2) that he may have to think awhile before he discovers what he "really" means by a given word, we are led to consider a test which will amount to a sort of Socratic questionnaire. That is, there will have to be prodding questions aimed at drawing the subject's attention to borderline cases, counterexamples, and various awkward consequences of his first and relatively off-hand answers. If as a result of these questions he is inclined to give a different answer from the one he gave at first, we may describe the phenomenon in various ways: we can say that he has changed his mind or learned something new, or we can say that he has now managed to find a better way of expressing what he really means (and perhaps has always meant) by the word. In general, it does not seem possible to differentiate in a practical way between *finding out* what someone means by a word, and *influencing* his linguistic behavior relative to that word. A philosopher who had been brought up on Plato might be inclined to think that when a group of persons were subjected to a Socratic interrogation their answers would at first be very diverse and later would tend to converge on one, or at most a few, definitions of the term in question. It would be interesting to know whether questionnaires could be designed which would have this effect, and also whether one could design a sort of anti-Socratic questionnaire which would tend to lead subjects to greater and greater disagreement.[11]

On the whole, it seems to me unwise, initially at least, to try to limit oneself either to the intensional or to the extensional approach. It will in practice be difficult to separate the two when one is designing a concrete test for determining the ordinary sense of a given word; they are rather to be thought of as different moments or tendencies which actual methods will combine in varying proportions. It could easily happen, however, as it has in certain well-known analogous cases, that experience would teach us to revise our conceptual framework, or at least to change our estimates of what is important and valuable.[12] It may turn out desirable to distinguish different senses of the expression "ordinary use,"

---

[11] If the latter were possible, it would obviously be awkward to interpret the Socratic method as a method of *finding out* what the subject means, as against *teaching* him something new.

[12] Thus, the concept of "definiteness of intention," introduced by Professor Arne Naess [cf. "Toward a Theory of Interpretation and Preciseness," in *Semantics and the Philosophy of Language,* L. Linsky, ed. (Urbana, Ill.: University of Illinois Press, 1952), pp. 256ff.], seems to have a devastating relevance to many of the characteristic assertions of the ordinary language philosophers.

corresponding to different methods of verifying statements in which this expression occurs, and one would then wish to know in which, if any, of these senses it would be true and important to say that in philosophic problems words do not have their ordinary use.

MUST WE MEAN

WHAT WE SAY?[1]

STANLEY CAVELL

That what we ordinarily say and mean may have a direct and deep control over what we can philosophically say and mean is an idea which many philosophers find oppressive. It might be argued that in part the oppression results from misunderstanding; that the new philosophy which proceeds from ordinary language is not *that* different from traditional methods of philosophizing, and that the frequent attacks upon it are

From Inquiry, *Vol. I (1958). Reprinted by permission of the author and the editor of* Inquiry.
[1] This is a later, greatly expanded, version of the paper read as part of the symposium mentioned in Mates' first note. Since writing the relevant portions of this paper, I have seen three articles which make points or employ arguments similar to those I am concerned with: R. M. Hare, "Are Discoveries About the Uses of Words Empirical?" *Journal of Philosophy,* Vol. LIV (1957); G. E. M. Anscombe, "On Brute Facts," *Analysis,* Vol. XVIII (1957-1958); S. Hampshire and H. L. A. Hart, "Decision, Intention and Certainty," *Mind,* Vol. LXVII (1958). But it would have lengthened an already lengthy paper to have tried to bring out more specifically than will be obvious to anyone reading them their relevance to what I have said.

misdirected. But I shall not attempt to be conciliatory, both because I think the new philosophy at Oxford is critically different from traditional philosophy, and because I think it is worth trying to bring out their differences as fully as possible. There *is,* after all, something oppressive about a philosophy which seems to have uncanny information about our most personal philosophical assumptions (those, for example, about whether we can ever know for certain of the existence of the external world, or of other minds; and those we make about favorite distinctions between "the descriptive and the normative," or between matters of fact and matters of language) and which inveterately nags us about them. Particularly oppressive when that philosophy seems so often *merely* to nag and to try no special answers to the questions which possess us—unless it be to suggest that we sit quietly in a room. Eventually, I suppose, we will have to look at that sense of oppression itself: such feelings can come from a truth about ourselves which we are holding off.

My hopes here are modest. I shall want to say why, in my opinion, some of the arguments Professor Mates brings against the Oxford philosophers he mentions are on the whole irrelevant to their main concerns. And this will require me to say something about what I take to be the significance of proceeding, in one's philosophizing, from what we ordinarily say and mean. That will not be an easy thing to do without appearing alternately trivial and dogmatic. Perhaps that is only to be expected, given the depth and the intimacy of conflict between this way of proceeding in philosophy and the way I take Mates to be following. These ways of philosophy seem, like friends who have quarreled, to be able neither to tolerate nor to ignore one another. I shall frequently be saying something one could not fail to know; and that will appear trivial. I shall also be suggesting that something we know is being overemphasized and something else not taken seriously enough; and that will appear dogmatic. But since I am committed to this dialogue, the time is past for worrying about appearances.

Professor Mates is less concerned to dispute specific results of the Oxford philosophers than he is to question the procedures which have led these philosophers to claim them. In particular, he doubts that they have assembled the sort of evidence which their "statements about ordinary language" require. As a basis for his skepticism, Mates produces a disagreement between two major figures of the school over the interpretation of an expression of ordinary language—a disagreement which he regards as symptomatic of the shallowness of their methods.[2] On

---

[2] I am too conscious of differences in the practices of Oxford philosophers to be happy about referring, in this general way, to a school. But nothing in my remarks depends on the existence of such a school—beyond the fact that certain

Mates' account of it, the conflict is not likely to be settled successfully by further discussion. We are faced with two professors (of philosophy, it happens) each arguing (claiming, rather) that the way he talks is the right way and that what he intuits about language is the truth about it. But if this is what their claims amount to, it hardly seems worth a philosopher's time to try to collect evidence for them.

To evaluate the disagreement between Austin and Ryle, we may distinguish among the statements they make about ordinary language, three types:[3] (1) There are statements which produce *instances* of what is said in a language ("We do say . . . but we don't say—"; "We ask whether . . . but we do not ask whether—"); (2) Sometimes these instances are accompanied by *explications*—statements which make explicit what is implied when we say what statements of the first type instance us as saying ("When we say . . . we imply (suggest, say)—"; "We don't say . . . unless we mean—"). Such statements are checked by reference to statements of the first type. (3) Finally, there are *generalizations,* to be tested by reference to statements of the first two types. Since there is no special problem here about the testing of generalizations, we will be concerned primarily with the justification of statements of the first two types, and especially with the second.

Even without attempting to be more precise about these differences, the nature of the clash between Ryle and Austin becomes somewhat clearer. Notice, first of all, that the statement Mates quotes from Austin is of the first type: "Take 'voluntarily' . . . : we may . . . make a gift voluntarily . . ."—which I take to be material mode for, "We say, 'The gift was made voluntarily.'" (The significance of this shift of "mode" will be discussed.) Only one of the many statements Mates quotes from Ryle is of this type, viz., "It makes sense . . . to ask whether a boy was responsible for breaking a window, but not whether he was responsible for finishing his homework in good time. . . ." The statements of Ryle's which clash with Austin's are different: "In their most ordinary employment 'voluntary' and 'involuntary' are used . . . as adjectives applying to actions which ought not to be done. We discuss whether someone's action was voluntary or not only when the action seems to have been his fault . . . etc." These do not produce *instances* of what we say (the way "We say 'The boy was responsible for breaking the window'" does); they are generalizations—as the phrases "actions which" and "only when" show—to be tested by producing such instances.

---

problems are common to the philosophers mentioned, and that similar questions enter into their attempts to deal with them. It is with these questions (I mean, of course, with what I understand them to be) that I am concerned.

[3] Perhaps I should say "ideal" types. The statements do not come labeled in the discourse of such philosophers, but I am going to have to trust that my placing of statements into these types will not seem to distort them.

It is true that the instance quoted from Austin does go counter to Ryle's generalization: making a gift is not always something which ought not to be done, or something which is always someone's fault. There is clearly a clash here. But is our only intelligent course *at this point* to take a poll? Would it be dogmatic or unempirical of us to conclude simply that Ryle is wrong about this, that he has settled upon a generalization to which an obvious counterinstance has been produced? It is, moreover, an instance which Ryle himself may well be expected to acknowledge as counter to his generalization; indeed, one which he might have produced for himself. The fact that he did not need indicate only that he was too quick to accept a generalization, not that he is without (good) evidence for it. One of Mates' objections to Ryle can be put this way: Ryle *is* without evidence—anyway, without very good evidence—because he is not entitled to a statement of the first type (one which presents an *instance* of what we say) in the absence of experimental studies which demonstrate its occurrence in the language.

To see that this objection, taken in the general sense in which Mates urges it, is groundless, we must bear in mind the fact that these statements—statements that something is said in English—are being made by native speakers of English. Such speakers do not, in *general,* need evidence for what is said in the language; they are the source of such evidence. It is from them that the descriptive linguist takes the corpus of utterances on the basis of which he will construct a grammar of that language. To answer *some* kinds of specific questions, we will have to engage in that "laborious questioning" Mates insists upon, and count noses; but in general, to tell what is and isn't English, and to tell whether what is said is properly used, the native speaker can rely on his own nose; if not, there would be nothing to count. No one speaker will say everything, so it may be profitable to seek out others; and sometimes you (as a native speaker) may be unsure that a form of utterance is as you say it is, or is used as you say it is used, and in that case you will have to check with another native speaker. And because attending so hard to what you say may itself make you unsure more often than is normal, it is a good policy to check more often. A good policy, but not a methodological necessity. The philosopher who proceeds from ordinary language, in his use of himself as subject in his collection of data, may be more informal than the descriptive linguist (though not more than the linguistic theorist using examples from his native speech); but there is nothing in that to make the data, in some general way, suspect.

Nor does this imply a reliance on that "intuition or memory" which Mates (p. 68) finds so objectionable. In claiming to know, in general, whether we do or do not use a given expression, I am not claiming to have an infallible memory for what we say, any more than I am claiming to remember the hour when I tell you what time we have dinner on

Sundays. A normal person may forget and remember certain words, or what certain words mean, in his native language, but (assuming that he has used it continuously) he does not remember the *language*. There is a world of difference between a person who speaks a language natively and one who knows the language fairly well. If I lived in Munich and knew German fairly well, I might try to intuit or guess what the German expression for a particular phenomenon is. Or I might ask my landlady; and that would probably be the extent of the laborious questioning the problem demanded. Nor does the making of either of the sorts of statement about ordinary language I have distinguished rely on a claim that "[we have] already amassed . . . a tremendous amount of empirical information about the use of [our] native language" (Mates, *ibid*.). That would be true if we were, say, making statements about the history of the language, or about its sound system, or about the housewife's understanding of political slogans, or about a special form in the morphology of some dialect. But for a native speaker to say what, in ordinary circumstances, is said when, no such special information is needed or claimed. All that is needed is the truth of the proposition that a natural language is what native speakers of that language speak.

Ryle's generalization, however, requires more than simple, first level statements of instances; it also requires statements of the second type, those which contain first level statements together with an "explication" of them. When Ryle claims that ". . . we raise questions of responsibility only when someone is charged, justly or unjustly, with an offence," he is claiming both, "We say 'The boy was responsible for breaking a window,' but we do not say 'The boy was responsible for finishing his homework in good time,' " and also claiming, "When we say 'The boy was responsible for (some action)' we imply that the action was an offence, one that ought not to have been done, one that was his fault." I want to argue that Ryle is, in general, as entitled to statements of this second type as he is to statements of the first type; although it is just here that the particular generalization in question misses. We know Austin's example counters Ryle's claim because we know that the statement (of the second type), "When we say, 'The gift was made voluntarily' we imply that the action of making the gift was one which ought not to be done, or was someone's fault" is false. This is clearly knowledge which Mates was relying on when he produced the clash between them. I will take up statements of the second type in a moment.

Before proceeding to that, let us look at that clash a bit longer: its importance has altered considerably. What Austin says does not go fully counter to Ryle's story. It is fundamental to Austin's account to emphasize that we cannot *always* say of actions that they were voluntary, even when they obviously were not involuntary either. Although we can (sometimes) say, "The gift was made voluntarily," it is specifically not something we can say about ordinary, unremarkable cases of making gifts. Only when the action (or circumstances) of making the gift is in some way unusual (instead of his usual Christmas bottle, you give the neighborhood policeman a check for $1000), or extraordinary (you leave your heirs penniless and bequeath your house to your cat), or untoward (you give your rocking horse to your new friend, but the next morning you cry to have it back), can the question whether it was voluntary intelligibly arise. Ryle has not completely neglected this: his "actions which ought not be done" and his "action [which] seems to have been . . . [someone's] fault" are clearly examples of actions which are abnormal, untoward, questionable; so he is right in saying that about these we (sometimes) raise the question whether they were voluntary. His error lies in characterizing these actions incompletely, and in wrongly characterizing those about which the question *cannot* arise. Normally, it is true, the question whether satisfactory, correct, or admirable performances are voluntary does not arise; but this is because there is usually nothing about such actions to question; nothing has gone wrong.

Not seeing that the condition for applying the term "voluntary" holds quite generally—viz., the condition that there be something (real or imagined) fishy about any performance intelligibly so characterized—Ryle construes the condition too narrowly, supposes that there must be something *morally* fishy about the performance. He had indeed sensed trouble where trouble was: the philosophical use of "voluntary" stretches the idea of volition out of shape, beyond recognition. And his diagnosis of the trouble was sound: philosophers imagine, because of a distorted picture of the mind, that the term "voluntary" must apply to all actions which are not involuntary (or unintentional), whereas it is only applicable where there is some specific reason to raise the question. The fact that Ryle fails to specify its applicability precisely enough no more vitiates his entire enterprise than does the fact that he indulges a mild form of the same vice he describes: he frees himself of the philosophical tic of stretching what is true of definite segments of what we do to cover *everything* we do (as epistemologists stretch doubt to cover everything we say), but not from the habit of identifying linguistic antitheses with logical contradictories:[4] in particular, he takes the question, "Voluntary or not?" to mean, "Voluntary or involuntary?" and seems to suppose that (responsible) actions which are not contemptible must be admirable,

---

[4] The harmfulness of this habit is brought out in Austin's "A Plea for Excuses." (See above, pp. 52ff.) Pages 46ff. of this paper contain an elaborate defense of (anyway Austin's version of) "ordinary language philosophy." No one concerned with the general subject of the present symposium (or, in particular, with the possibility of budging the subject of moral philosophy) should (= will) neglect its study.

and that whatever I (responsibly) do either is my fault or else is to my credit. These antitheses miss exactly those actions about which the question "Voluntary or not?" really has no sense, viz., those ordinary, unremarkable, natural things we do which make up most of our conduct and which are neither admirable nor contemptible; which, indeed, could only erroneously be said to go on, in general, in *any* special way.[5] Lacking firmness here, it is not surprising that Ryle's treatment leaves the subject a bit wobbly. Feeling how *enormously* wrong it is to remove "voluntary" from a *specific* function, he fails to sense the slighter error of his own specification.[6]

I have said that the ordinary language philosopher is also and equally entitled to statements of the second type I distinguished, which means that he is entitled not merely to say what (words) we say, but equally to say what we should mean in (by) saying them. Let us turn to statements of this type and ask what the relation is between what you explicitly say and what you imply; or, to avoid begging the question, ask how we are to account for the fact (supposing it to be a fact) that we only say or ask A ("X is voluntary," or "Is X voluntary?") where B is the case (something is, or seems, fishy about X).[7] The philosophical problem about this arises in the following way: Philosophers who proceed from ordinary language are likely to insist that if you say A where B is not the case, you will be misusing A, or distorting its meaning. But another philosopher will not want to allow that, because it makes the

---

[5] Austin's discovery (for our time and place, anyway) of normal action is, I think, important enough to bear the philosophical weight he puts upon it — holding the clue to the riddle of Freedom. (See above, p. 45.) A case can also be made out that it was failure to recognize such action which produced some of the notorious paradoxes of classical Utilitarianism: what neither the Utilitarians nor their critics seem to have seen clearly and constantly is that about unquestionable (normal, natural) action no question is (can be) raised; in particular not the question whether the action ought or ought not to have been done. The point is a logical one: to raise a question about an action is to put the action in question. It is partly the failure to appreciate this which makes the classical moralists (appear?) so moralistic, allows them to suppose that the moral question is *always* appropriate [except, of course, where the action is unfree (caused?)]. But this is no better than the assumption that the moral question is *never* appropriate (because we are never *really* free). Such mechanical moralism has got all the punishment it deserves in the recent mechanical antimoralism, which it must have helped inspire.

[6] At the same time, Ryle leaves "involuntary" as stretched as ever when he allows himself to speak of "the involuntariness of [someone's] late arrival" [*The Concept of Mind* (London: Hutchinson and Co., Ltd., 1949), p. 72].

[7] I realize that the point is controversial and that in putting so much emphasis on it I may be doing some injustice to the point of view I am trying to defend. There may be considerations which would lead one to be more temperate in making the point; but against the point of view Mates is adopting, it seems to me to demand all the attention it can get.

relation between A and B appear to be a logical one (If A then B; and if not-B then not-A); whereas logical relations hold only between statements, not between a statement and the world: *that* relation is "merely" conventional (or, even, causal?). So the occasion on which we (happen to?) *use* a statement cannot be considered part of its meaning or logic. The solution is then to call the latter the semantics of the expression and the former its pragmatics.

But if we can forget for a moment that the relation between A and B *cannot* be a logical one, we may come to feel how implausible it is to *say* that it is not logical; or rather, to say that nothing *follows* about B from the utterance of A. It is implausible because we do not accept a question like "Did you do that voluntarily?" as appropriate about any and every action. If a person asks you whether you dress the way you do voluntarily, you will not understand him to be curious merely about your psychological processes (whether your wearing them "proceeds from free choice . . .") ; you will understand him to be implying or suggesting that your manner of dress is in some way peculiar. If it be replied to this that "voluntary" does not *mean* "peculiar" (or "special" or "fishy") and hence that the implication or suggestion is part merely of the pragmatics of the expression, not part of its *meaning* (semantics), my rejoinder is this: that reply is relevant to a different claim from the one urged here; it is worth saying *here* only if you are able to account for the *relation* between the pragmatics and the semantics of the expression. In the absence of such an account, the reply is empty. For consider: If we use Mates' formula for computing the pragmatic value of an expression—"He wouldn't say that unless he . . ."—then in the described situation we will complete it with something like ". . . unless he thought that my way of dressing is peculiar." Call this implication of the utterance "pragmatic"; the fact remains that he wouldn't (couldn't) say what he did without implying what he did: he MUST MEAN that my clothes are peculiar. I am less interested now in the "mean" than I am in the "must." (After all, there is bound to be some reason why a number of philosophers are tempted to call a relation logical; "must" is logical.) But on this, the "pragmatic" formula throws no light whatever.

What this shows is that the formula does not help us account for the element of necessity ("must") in statements whose implication we understand. But it is equally unhelpful in trying to explain the implication of a statement whose use we do *not* understand (the context in which the formula enters Mates' discussion). Imagine that I am sitting in my countinghouse counting up my money. Someone who knows that I do that at this hour every day passes by and says, "You ought to do that." What should we say about his statement? That he does not know what "ought" means (what the dictionary says)? That he does not know how to use the word? That he does not know what obligation is? Applying the formula, we compute: "He wouldn't say that unless he asks himself whenever he sees anyone doing anything, 'Ought that person to be doing that or ought he not?'" This may indeed account for his otherwise puzzling remark; but it does so by telling us something we did not know about *him;* it tells us nothing whatever we did not know about the words he used. Here it is *because* we know the meaning and use of "ought" that we are forced to account in the way Mates suggests for its extraordinary occurrence. I take Mates' formula, then, to be expandable into: "Since I understand the meaning and use of his expression, he wouldn't say that unless he. . . ." Perhaps Mates would consider this a distortion and take a different expansion to be appropriate: "He wouldn't say that unless he was using his words in a special way." But now "say that" has a very different force. The expanded form now means, "I know what his expression would ordinarily be used to say, but he can't wish to say that: I don't understand what he is saying." In neither of its expansions, then, does the formula throw any light on the way an expression is being used: in the one case we already know, in the other we have yet to learn. (Another expansion may be: "He wouldn't say that unless he was using X to mean Y." But here again, it is the semantics and pragmatics of Y which are relevant to understanding what is said, and the formula presupposes that we already understand Y.)

Our alternatives seem to be these: Either (1) we deny that there is any rational (logical, grammatical) constraint over the "pragmatic implications" of what we say—or perhaps deny that there *are* any *implications,* on the ground that the relation in question is not deductive— so that unless what I say is flatly false or unless I explicitly contradict myself, it is pointless to suggest that what I say is wrong or that I must mean something other than I say; or else (2) we admit the constraint and say either (a) since all necessity is logical, the "pragmatic implications" of our utterance are (quasi-)logical implications; with or without adding (b) since the "pragmatic implications" cannot be construed in terms of deductive (or inductive) logic, there must be some "third sort" of logic; or we say (c) some necessity is not logical. None of these alternatives is without its obscurities, but they are clear enough for us to see that Mates is taking alternative (1),[8] whereas the philosopher who proceeds from ordinary language is likely to feel the need of some form

---

[8] As is most clearly shown where he says (p. 72) ". . . When I say 'I may be wrong' I do not *imply* that I have no confidence in what I have previously asserted; I only indicate it." Why "only"? Were he willing to say ". . . but I do (inevitably) indicate it," there may be no argument.

of (2). Alternative (2a) brings out part of the reason behind the Oxford philosopher's insistence that he is talking logic, while (2b) makes explicit the reason other philosophers are perplexed at that claim.[9]

The difference between alternatives (1) and (2) is fundamental; so fundamental, that it is very difficult to argue. When Mates says, "Perhaps it is true that ordinarily I wouldn't say 'I know it' unless I felt great confidence in what I was asserting . . . ," what he says is not, if you like, *strictly* wrong; but it is wrong—or, what it implies is wrong. It implies that whether I confine the formula "I know . . ." to statements about which I feel great confidence is *up to me* (*rightly* up to me); so that if I say "I know . . ." in the absence of confidence, I have not misused language, and in particular I have not stretched the *meaning* of the word "know." And yet, if a child were to say "I know . . ." when you know the child does not *know* (is in no position to say he knows) you may reply, "You don't really mean (N.B.) you *know*, you only mean you believe"; or you may say, "You oughtn't to say you *know* when you only *think* so."

There are occasions on which it would be useful to have the "semantic-pragmatic" distinction at hand. If, for example, a philosopher tells me that the statement, "You ought to do so-and-so" expresses private emotion and is hortatory and hence not, strictly speaking, meaningful, then it may be worth replying that nothing follows about the meaning (semantics) of a statement from the way it is used (pragmatics); and this reply may spare our having to make up special brands of meaning. But the time for that argument is, presumably, past.[10] What needs to be argued now is that something *does* follow from the fact that a term is used in its usual way: it entitles you (or, using the term, you entitle others) to make certain inferences, draw certain conclusions. (This is part of what you say when you say that you are talking about the *logic* of ordinary language.) *Learning what these implications are is part of learning the language;* no less a part than learning its syntax, or learning what it is to which terms apply: they are an essential part of what we communicate when we talk. Intimate understanding is understanding which is implicit. Nor *could* everything we say (mean to communicate),

---

[9] Alternative (2b) has been taken—for different, but not unrelated, reasons—in the writings of John Wisdom [e.g., "Gods," in *Logic and Language,* 1st series, Antony Flew, ed. (Oxford: Basil Blackwell & Mott, Ltd., 1951), p. 196], in S. Toulmin, *The Place of Reason in Ethics* (London: Cambridge University Press, 1950), p. 83, and in S. Hampshire, "Fallacies in Moral Philosophy," *Mind,* Vol. LVIII (1949), 470f.

[10] It was essentially the argument with which the pragmatists attempted to subdue emotive "meaning." See John Dewey, "Ethical Subject-Matter and Language," *Journal of Philosophy,* Vol. XLII (1945), 701ff.

in normal communication, be said explicitly[11]—otherwise the only threat to communication would be acoustical. We are, therefore, exactly as responsible for the specific implications of our utterances as we are for their explicit factual claims. And there can no more be some general procedure for securing that what one implies is appropriate than there can be for determining that what one says is true. Misnaming and misdescribing are not the only mistakes we can make in talking. Nor is lying its only immorality.

I am prepared to conclude that the philosopher who proceeds from ordinary language is entitled, without special empirical investigation, to assertions of the second sort we distinguished, viz., assertions like, "We do not say 'I know . . .' unless we mean that we have great confidence . . . ," and like "When we ask whether an action is voluntary we imply that the action is fishy" (call this S). But I do not think that I have *shown* that he is entitled to them, because I have not shown what kind of assertions they are; I have not shown when such assertions should be said, and by whom, and what should be meant in saying them. It is worth trying to indicate certain complexities of the assertions, because they are easy to overlook. Something important will be learned if we realize that we do *not* know what kind of assertion S is.

When (if) you feel that S is necessarily true, that it is a priori, you will have to explain how a statement which is obviously not analytic *can* be true a priori. [That S is not analytic is what (is all) that is shown by Mates' arguments about the "semantic-pragmatic" confusion;

---

[11] I think of this as a law of communication; but it would be important and instructive to look for apparent counterinstances. When *couldn't* what is said be misunderstood? My suggestion is, only when nothing is implied, i.e., when everything you say is said explicitly. (Should we add, or when all of the implications of what is asserted can be made explicit *in a certain way*, e.g., by the methods of formal logic? It may be along such lines that utterances in logical form come to seem the ideal of understandable utterances, that here you can communicate *only* what you say, or else *more* than you say without endangering understanding. But we might think of formal logic not as the guarantor of understanding but as a substitute for it. [Cf. W. V. O. Quine, "Mr. Strawson on Logical Theory," *Mind*, Vol. LXII (1953), 444f.] Then we can express this "law of communication" this way: What needs understanding can be misunderstood.) But when *is* everything said explicitly? When the statement is about sense-data rather than "physical" objects? When it is about the (physical) movements I make rather than the (nonphysical?) actions I perform? Perhaps the opponents of the Quest for Certainty (whose passion seems to have atrophied into a fear of the word "certain") have embarked upon a Quest for Explicitness. Strawson's notion of *presupposing* is relevant here, since explicitness and presupposition vary inversely. See "On Referring," *Mind*, Vol. LIX (1950); reprinted in *Essays in Conceptual Analysis*, Antony Flew, ed. (London: Macmillan & Co., Ltd., 1956).

it is perfectly true that "voluntary" does not *mean* (you will not find set beside it in a dictionary) "fishy."] When I am impressed with the necessity of statements like S, I am tempted to say that they are categorial—about the concept of an action *überhaupt*. (A normal action is neither voluntary nor involuntary, neither careful nor careless, neither expected nor unexpected, neither right nor wrong. . . .) This would account for our feeling of their necessity: they are instances (not of Formal, but) of Transcendental Logic. But this is really no explanation until we make clearer the need for the concept of an action in general.

However difficult it is to make out a case for the necessity of S, it is important that the temptation to call it a priori not be ignored; otherwise we will acquiesce in calling it synthetic, which would be badly misleading. Misleading (wrong) because we know what would count as a disproof of statements which are synthetic (to indicate the willingness to entertain such disproof is the point of calling a statement synthetic), but it is not clear what would count as a disproof of S. The feeling that S must be synthetic comes, of course, partly from the fact that it obviously is not (likely to be taken as) analytic. But it comes also from the ease with which S may be mistaken for the statement, " 'Is X voluntary?' implies that X is fishy" (T), which does seem obviously synthetic. But S and T, though they are true together and false together, are not everywhere interchangeable; the identical state of affairs is described by both, but a person who may be entitled to say T, may not be entitled to say S. Only a native speaker of English is entitled to the statement S, whereas a linguist describing English may, though he is not a native speaker of English, be entitled to T. What entitles him to T is his having gathered a certain amount and kind of evidence in its favor. But the person entitled to S is not entitled to *that* statement for the same reason. He *needs* no evidence for it. It would be misleading to say that he *has* evidence for S, for that would suggest that he has done the sort of investigation the linguist has done, only less systematically, and this would make it seem that his claim to know S is very weakly based. And it would be equally misleading to say that he does *not* have evidence for S, because that would make it appear that there is something he still needs, and suggests that he is not yet entitled to S. But there is nothing he needs, and there is no evidence (which it makes sense, in *general,* to say) he has: the question of evidence is irrelevant.

An examination of what does entitle a person to the statement S would be required in any full account of such statements. Such an examination is out of the question here. But since I will want to claim that Mates' "two methods" for gathering evidence in support of "statements about ordinary language" like S are irrelevant to what entitles a person to S, and since this obviously rests on the claim that the concept of evidence is, in general, irrelevant to them altogether, let me say just this: The clue to understanding the sort of statement S is lies in appreciating the fact that "we," while plural, is first person. First person *singular* forms have recently come in for a great deal of attention, and they have been shown to have very significant logical-epistemological properties. The plural form has similar, and equally significant, properties; but it has been, so far as I know, neglected. The claim that in general we do not require evidence for statements in the first person plural does not rest upon a claim that we cannot be wrong about what we are doing or about what we say, but only that it would be extraordinary if we were (often). My point about such statements, then, is that they are sensibly questioned only where there is some special reason for supposing what I say about what I (we) say to be wrong; only here is the request for evidence competent. If I am wrong about what he does (they do), that may be no great surprise; but if I am wrong about what I (we) do, that is liable, where it is not comic, to be tragic.

Statements like T have their own complexities, and it would be unwise even of them to say simply that they are synthetic. Let us take another of Mates' examples: " 'I know it' is not (ordinarily) said unless the speaker has great confidence in it" (T'). Mates takes this as patently synthetic, a statement about matters of fact (and there is no necessary connection among matters of fact). And so it might be, said by a Scandinavian linguist as part of his description of English. But if that linguist, or if a native speaker (i.e., a speaker entitled to say, "We do not say 'I know it' unless . . .") uses T' in teaching someone to speak English, or to remind a native speaker of something he knows but is not bearing in mind, T' sounds less like a descriptive statement than like a rule.

Because of what seems to be the widespread idea that rules always sort with commands and must therefore be represented as imperatives, this complementarity of rule and statement may come as something of a shock. But that such complementarity exists can be seen in writings which set out the rules for games or ceremonies or languages. In *Hoyle's Rules of Games* we find statements like, "The opponent at declarer's left makes the opening lead . . . Declarer's partner then lays his whole hand face up on the table, with his trumps if any on the right. The hand so exposed is the *dummy*. . . . The object of play is solely to win tricks, in order to fulfill or defeat the contract"; in Robert's Rules of Order, the rules take the form, "The privileged motion to adjourn takes precedence of all others, except the privileged motion 'to fix the time to which to adjourn,' to which it yields" (in Section 17, headed "To Adjourn") ; taking a grammar at random we find, "Mute stems form the nominative singular by the addition of -s in the case of masculines and feminines . . . Before -s of the nominative singular, a labial mute (p, b) remains unchanged." These are all statements in the indicative, not the imperative, mood. (Some expressions in each of these books tell us what we *must* do; others that we *may*. I will suggest later a reason for this shift.) In one light, they appear to be descriptions; in another to be rules. Why should this be so? What is its significance?

The explanation of the complementarity has to do with the fact that its topic is actions. When we say how an action is done (how to act) what we say may report or describe the way we *in fact* do it (if we are entitled to say how "we" do it, i.e, to say what we do, or say what we say) but it may also lay out a way of doing or saying something which is to be *followed*. Whether remarks like T′—remarks "about" ordinary language, and equally about ordinary actions—are statements or rules depends upon how they are taken: if they are taken to state facts and are supposed to be believed, they are statements; if they are taken as guides and supposed to be followed, they are rules. Such expressions are no more "in themselves" rules or (synthetic) statements than other expressions are, in themselves, postulates or conclusions or definitions or replies. We might put the relation between the two contexts of T′ this way: Statements which describe a language (or a game or an institution) are rules (are binding) if you want to speak that language (play that game, accept that institution); or, rather, *when* you are speaking that language, playing that game, etc. *If it is* TRUE *to say "'I know it' is not used unless you have great confidence in it," then, when you are speaking English, it is* WRONG (*a misuse*) *to say "I know it" unless you have great confidence in it.* Now the philosopher who proceeds from ordinary language assumes that he and his interlocutors are speaking from within the language, so that the question of whether you want to speak that language is pointless. Worse than pointless, because strictly the ordinary language philosopher does not, in general, *assume* that he and his interlocutors are speaking from within a given (their native) language—any more than they speak their native language, in general, *intentionally*. The only condition relevant to such philosophizing is that you speak (not this or that language, but) period.

At this point the argument has become aporetic. "Statements about ordinary language" like S, T and T′ are not analytic, *and* they are not (it would be misleading to call them) synthetic (just like that).[12] Nor

---

[12] If it still seems that statements like S and T *must* be synthetic, perhaps it will help to realize that anyway they are not *just some more* synthetic statements about voluntary action, on a par with a statement to the effect that somebody does (indeed) dress the way he does voluntarily. It may be true that if the world were different *enough,* the statements would be false; but that amounts to saying that if "voluntary" meant something other than it does, the statements would not mean what they do—which is not surprising. The statements in question are more closely related to such a statement as "The future will resemble the past": this is not a (not just another) prediction, on a par with statements about whether it will rain. Russell's chicken (who was fed every

do we know whether to say they are a priori, or whether to account for their air of necessity as a dialectical illusion, due more to the motion of our argument than to their own nature. Given our current alternatives, there is no way to classify such statements; we do not yet know what they are.

Before searching for new ways into these problems, I should perhaps justify my very heavy reliance on the idea of *context,* because on Mates' description of what a statement of context involves, it should be impossible ever to make one. Let me recall his remarks: "We have all heard the wearying platitude that 'you can't separate' the meaning of a word from the entire context in which it occurs, including not only the actual linguistic context, but also the aims, feelings, beliefs, and hopes of the speaker, the same for the listener and any bystanders, the social situation, the physical surroundings, the historical background, the rules of the game, and so on ad infinitum" (p. 71). Isn't this another of those apostrophes to the infinite which prevents philosophers from getting down to cases? [13] Of course if I have to go on about the context of "voluntary" ad infinitum, I would not get very far with it. But I would claim to have characterized the context sufficiently (for the purpose at hand) by the statement that something is, or is supposed to be, fishy about the action. Giving directions for using a word is no more prodigious and unending a task than giving directions for anything else. The context in which I make a martini with vodka is no less complex than the context in which I make a statement with "voluntary." Say, if you like, that these actions take place in infinitely complex contexts; but then remember that you can be given directions for doing either. It may be wearying always to be asked for a story within which a puzzling remark can seriously be imagined to function; but I know no better way of maintaining that relevance, or sense of reality, which each philosopher claims for himself and claims to find lacking in another philosophy. At least it would spare us the surrealism of worries like " 'What time is it?' asserts nothing, and hence is neither true nor false;

---

day throughout its life but ultimately had its neck wrung) was so well fed that he neglected to consider what was happening to other chickens. Even if he had considered this, he would doubtless still have had his neck wrung; but at least he wouldn't have been outsmarted. He could have avoided *that* indignity because he was wrong only about one thing; as Russell very properly says, ". . . in spite of frequent repetitions there sometimes is a failure at the last" [*The Problems of Philosophy* (London: Oxford University Press, 1912), p. 102]. But if the future were not (in the *general* sense needed) "like" the past, this would not be *a* failure. The future may wring our minds, but by that very act it would have given up trying to outsmart us.

[13] A complaint Austin voiced in the course of his William James Lectures, on Performatives, at Harvard in the Spring term of 1955.

yet we all know what it means *well enough* to answer it";[14] or like "If we told a person to close the door, and received the reply, 'Prove it!' should we not, to speak mildly, grow somewhat impatient?" [15]

In recommending that we ignore context in order to make "provisional divisions" of a subject and get an investigation started, Mates is recommending the wrong thing for the right reason. It is true that we cannot say everything at once and that for some problems some distinction of the sort Mates has in mind may be of service. My discontent with it is that it has come to deflect investigation—I mean from questions on which Oxford philosophy trains itself. Where your concern is one of constructing artificial languages, you may explain that you mean to be considering only the syntax (and perhaps semantics) of a language, and not its pragmatics. Or where it becomes important to emphasize a distinction between (where there has come to be a distinction between) scientific and metaphysical assertion, or between factual report and moral rule, you may set out a "theory" of scientific or factual utterance. In these cases you will be restricting concern in order to deal with certain properties of formal systems, certain problems of meaning, and to defeat certain forms of nonsense. Flat contradiction, metaphysical assertion masquerading as scientific hypothesis, mere whim under the posture of an ethical or aesthetic (or psychological or legal) judgment —these perhaps need hounding out. But the philosopher who proceeds from ordinary language is concerned less to avenge sensational crimes against the intellect than to redress its civil wrongs; to steady any imbalance, the tiniest usurpation, in the mind. This inevitably requires reintroducing ideas which have become tyrannical (e.g., existence, obligation, certainty, identity, reality, truth . . .) into the specific contexts in which they function naturally. This is not a question of cutting big ideas down to size, but of giving them the exact space in which they can move without corrupting. Nor does our wish to rehabilitate rather than to deny or expel such ideas (by such sentences as, "We can never know for certain . . ."; "The table is not real (really solid)"; "To tell me what I ought to do is always to tell me what you want me to do" . . .) come from a sentimental altruism. It is a question of self-preservation: for who is it that the philosopher punishes when it is the mind itself which assaults the mind?

I want now to turn to two other, related, questions on which Mates finds himself at issue with the Oxford philosophers. The first concerns their tendency to introduce statements of the first sort I distinguished

---

[14] John Hospers, *An Introduction to Philosophical Analysis* (Englewood Cliffs, N.J.: Prentice-Hall, Inc., 1953), p. 69. My emphasis.

[15] Charles Stevenson, *Ethics and Language* (New Haven: Yale University Press, 1944), p. 26.

not with "We do say . . ." but with "We *can* say . . ." and "We *can't* say. . . ." The second question concerns, at last directly, reasons for saying that we "must" mean by our words what those words *ordinarily* mean.

Let me begin by fulfilling my promise to expand upon my remark that Austin's saying, "We may make a gift voluntarily" is "material mode" for "We can say, 'The gift was made voluntarily.' " The shift from talking about language to talking about the world occurs almost imperceptibly in the statement of Austin's which Mates quotes—almost as though he thought it did not much matter *which* he talked about. Let me recall the passage from Austin: ". . . take 'voluntarily' and 'involuntarily': we may join the army or make a gift voluntarily, we may hiccough or make a small gesture involuntarily." He begins here by mentioning a pair of words, and goes on to tell us what we may in fact do. With what right? Why is it assumed that we find out what voluntary and involuntary actions *are* (and equally, of course, what inadvertent and automatic and pious, etc., actions are) by asking when we should *say* of an action that it is voluntary or inadvertent or pious, etc.?

But what is troubling about this? If you feel that finding out what something is must entail investigation of the world rather than of language, perhaps you are imagining a situation like finding out what somebody's name and address are, or what the contents of a will or a bottle are, or whether frogs eat butterflies. But now imagine that you are in your armchair reading a book of reminiscences and come across the word "umiak." You reach for your dictionary and look it up. Now what did you do? Find out what "umiak" means, or find out what an umiak is? But how could we have discovered something about the world by hunting in the dictionary? If this seems surprising, perhaps it is because we forget that we learn language and learn the world *together,* that they become elaborated and distorted together, and in the same places. We may also be forgetting how elaborate a process the learning is. We tend to take what a native speaker does when he looks up a noun in a dictionary as the characteristic process of learning language. (As, in what has become a less forgivable tendency, we take naming as the fundamental source of meaning.) But it is merely the end point in the process of learning the word. When we turned to the dictionary for "umiak" we already knew everything about the word, as it were, but its combination: we knew what a noun is and how to name an object and how to look up a word and what boats are and what an Eskimo is. We were all prepared for that umiak. What seemed like finding the world in a dictionary was really a case of bringing the world to the dictionary. We had the world with us all the time, in that armchair; but we felt the weight of it only when we felt a lack in it. Sometimes we will need to bring the dictionary to the world. That will happen when (say) we run across a small boat in Alaska of a sort we have never seen and wonder—what? What it is, or what it is called? In either case, the learning is a question of aligning language and the world.[16] What you need to learn will depend on what specifically it is you want to know; and how you can find out will depend specifically on what you already command. How we answer the question, "What is X?" will depend, therefore, on the specific case of ignorance and of knowledge.

It sometimes happens that we know everything there is to know about a situation—what all of the words in question mean, what all of the relevant facts are; and everything is in front of our eyes. And yet we feel we don't know something, don't understand something. In this situation, the question "What is X?" is very puzzling, in exactly the way philosophy is very puzzling. We feel we want to ask the question, and yet we feel we already have the answer. (One might say we have all the *elements* of an answer.) Socrates says that in such a situation we need to remind ourselves of something. So does the philosopher who proceeds from ordinary language: we need to remind ourselves of *what we should say when*.[17] But what is the point of reminding ourselves of that? When the philosopher asks, "What should we say here?," what is meant is, "What would be the normal thing to say here?," or perhaps, "What is the most natural thing we could say here?" And the point of the question is this: answering it is sometimes the only way to tell— tell others and tell for ourselves—what the situation *is*.

Sometimes the only way to tell. But when? The nature of the Oxford philosopher's question, and the nature of his conception of philosophy, can be brought out if we turn the question upon itself, and thus remind ourselves of when it is we need to remind ourselves of what we should say when. Our question then becomes: When should we ask ourselves when we should (and should not) say "The x is F" in order to find out what an F(x) is? [For "The x is F" read "The action is voluntary (or pious)," or "The statement is vague (or false)," or "The question is

---

[16] For modern instruction in the complexities of this question, see Austin's and P. F. Strawson's contributions to the symposium, "Truth," *Proceedings of the Aristotelian Society,* Suppl. Vol. XXIV (1950); D. F. Pears, "Universals" and "Incompatibilities of Colours," both in *Logic and Language,* 2nd series, Antony Flew, ed. (Oxford: Basil Blackwell & Mott, Ltd., 1953); W. V. O. Quine, "Two Dogmas of Empiricism," *Philosophical Review,* Vol. LX (1951); reprinted in *From a Logical Point of View* (Cambridge, Mass.: Harvard University Press, 1953); and John Wisdom, papers collected in *Philosophy and Psycho-Analysis* (Oxford: Basil Blackwell & Mott, Ltd., 1953), especially "Philosophical Perplexity," "Metaphysics and Verification," and "Philosophy, Metaphysics and Psycho-Analysis."

[17] The emphasized formula is Austin's. (See above, p. 46.) Notice that the "should" cannot simply be replaced by "ought to," nor yet, I believe, simply replaced by "would." It will not, that is, yield its secrets to the question, "Descriptive or normative?"

misleading."] The answer suggested is: When you have to. When you have more facts than you know what to make of, or when you do not know what new facts would show. When, that is, you need a clear view of what you already know. When you need to do philosophy.[18] Euthyphro does not need to learn any new facts, yet he needs to learn something: you can say either that in the *Euthyphro* Socrates was finding out what "piety" means or finding out what piety is.

When the philosopher who proceeds from ordinary language tells us, "You can't say such-and-such," what he means is that you cannot say that *here* and communicate *this* situation to others, or understand it for yourself.[19] This is sometimes what he means by calling certain expressions "misuses" of language, and also makes clear the consequences of such expressions: they break our understanding. The normativeness which Mates felt, and which is certainly present, does not lie in the ordinary language philosopher's assertions *about* ordinary use; what is normative is exactly ordinary use itself.

The way philosophers have practiced with the word "normative" in recent years seems to me lamentable. But it is too late to avoid the word, so even though we cannot now embark on a diagnosis of the ills which caused its current use, or those which it has produced, it may be worth forewarning ourselves against the confusions most likely to distract us. The main confusions about the problem of "normativeness" I want to mention here are these: the idea (1) that descriptive utterances are opposed to normative utterances; and (2) that prescriptive utterances are (typical) instances of normative utterances.

We have touched upon these ideas in talking about rule-statement complementarity; here we touch them at a different point. In saying here that it is a confusion to speak of some general opposition between descriptive and normative utterances, I am not thinking primarily of the plain fact that rules have counterpart (descriptive) statements, but rather of the significance of that fact, viz., that what such statements describe are *actions* (and not, e.g., the *movements* of bodies, animate or

---

[18] This is part of the view of philosophy most consistently represented in and by the writings of John Wisdom. It derives from Wittgenstein.

[19] Of course you can *say* (the words), "When I ask whether an action is voluntary I do not imply that I think something is special about the action." You can say this, but then you may have difficulty showing the relevance of *this* "voluntary" to what people are worrying about when they ask whether a person's action was voluntary or whether our actions are ever voluntary. We might regard the Oxford philosopher's insistence upon ordinary language as an attempt to overcome (what has become) the self-imposed irrelevance of so much philosophy. In this they are continuing—while at the same time their results are undermining—the tradition of British Empiricism: being gifted pupils, they seem to accept and to assassinate with the same gesture.

inanimate). The most characteristic fact about actions is that they can —in various specific ways—go wrong, that they can be performed incorrectly. This is not, in any restricted sense, a moral assertion, though it points the moral of intelligent activity. And it is as true of describing as it is of calculating or of promising or plotting or warning or asserting or defining. . . . These are actions which we perform, and our successful performance of them depends upon our adopting and following the ways in which the action in question is done, upon what is normative for it. Descriptive statements, then, are not opposed to ones which are normative, but in fact presuppose them: we could not do the thing we call describing if language did not provide (we had not been taught) ways normative for describing.

The other point I wish to emphasize is this: if a normative utterance is one used to create or institute rules or standards, then prescriptive utterances are not examples of normative utterances. Establishing a norm is not telling us how we *ought* to perform an action, but telling us how the action *is* done, or how it is *to be* done.[20] Contrariwise, telling us what we ought to do is not instituting a norm to cover the case, but rather presupposes the existence of such a norm, i.e., presupposes that there is something to do which it would be correct to do here. Telling us what we ought to do may involve *appeal* to a pre-existent rule or standard, but it cannot constitute the establishment of that rule or standard. We may expect the retort here that it is just the *appeal* which is the sensitive normative spot, for what we are really doing when we appeal to a rule or standard is telling somebody that they ought to adhere to it. Perhaps this will be followed by the query "And suppose they don't accept the rule or standard to which you appeal, what then?" The retort is simply false. And to the query one may reply that this will not be the first time we have been tactless; nor can we, to avoid overstepping the bounds of relationship, follow every statement by ". . . if you accept the facts and the logic I do," nor every evaluation by ". . . if you accept the standards I do." Such cautions will finally suggest appending to everything we say ". . . if you mean by your words what I mean by mine." Here the pantomime of caution concludes. It is true that we sometimes appeal to standards which our interlocutor does not accept; but this does not in the least show that what we are there really doing is attempting to institute a standard (of our own). Nor does it in the least show that we are (merely) expressing our own opinion or feeling on the matter. We of course

---

[20] This latter distinction appears in two senses of the expression "establishing a rule or standard." In one it means finding what is in fact standard in certain instances. In the other it means founding what is to be standard for certain instances. "Settle" and "determine" have senses comparable to those of "establish."

may express our private opinion or feeling—we normally do so where it is not clear what (or that any) rule or standard fits the case at hand and where we are therefore not willing or able to appeal to any.

The practice of appealing to a norm can be abused, as can any other of our practices. Sometimes people appeal to a rule when we deserved more intimate attention from them. Just as sometimes people tell us what we ought to do when all they mean is that they want us to. But this is as much an abuse where the context is moral as it is where the context is musical ("You ought to accent the appoggiatura"), or scientific ("You ought to use a control group here"), or athletic ("You ought to save your wind on the first two laps"). Private persuasion (or personal appeal) is not the paradigm of ethical utterance, but represents the breakdown (or the transcending) of moral interaction. We can, too obviously, become morally inaccessible to one another; but to tell us that these are the moments which really constitute the moral life will only add confusion to pain.

If not, then, by saying what actions *ought* to be performed, how *do* we establish (or justify or modify or drop) rules or standards? What general answer can there be to this general question other than "In various ways, depending on the context?" Philosophers who have imagined that the question has one answer for all cases must be trying to assimilate the members of Football Commissions, of Child Development Research Teams, of University Committees on Entrance Requirements, of Bar Association Committees to Alter Legal Procedures, of Departments of Agriculture, of Bureaus of Standards, and of Essene Sects, all to one "sort" of person, doing one "sort" of thing, viz., establishing (or changing) rules and standards. Whereas the fact is that there are, in each case, different ways normative for accomplishing the particular normative tasks in question. It has in recent years been emphasized past acknowledgment that even justifications require justification. What now needs emphasizing is that (successfully) justifying a statement or an action is not (cannot be) justifying its justification.[21] The assumption that the appeal to a rule or standard is only justified where that rule

---

[21] It is perfectly possible to maintain that *any* "justifications" we offer for our conduct are now so obviously empty and grotesquely inappropriate that nothing we used to call a justification is any longer acceptable, and that the *immediate* questions which face us concern the ultimate ground of justification itself. We have heard about, if we have not seen, the breaking down of convention, the fission of traditional values. But it is not a Continental dread at the realization that our standards have no ultimate justification which lends to so much British and American moral philosophizing its hysterical quality. (Such philosophy has been able to take the death of God in its stride.) That quality comes, rather, from the assumption that the question of justifying cases is on a par with (appropriate in the same context as) the question of justifying norms.

or standard is simultaneously established or justified can only serve to make such appeal seem hypocritical (or anyway shaky) and the attempts at such establishment or justification seem tyrannical (or anyway arbitrary).

It would be important to understand why we have been able to overlook the complementarity of rule and statement and to be content always to sort rules with imperatives. Part of the reason for this comes from a philosophically inadequate (not to say disastrous) conception of action; but this inadequacy itself will demand an elaborate accounting. There is another sort of reason for our assumption that what is binding upon us must be an imperative; one which has to do with our familiar sense of alienation from established systems of morality, perhaps accompanied by a sense of distance from God. Kant tells us that a perfectly rational being does in fact (necessarily) conform to "the supreme principle of morality," but that we imperfectly rational creatures are necessitated *by* it, so that for us it is (always appears as) an imperative. But if I understand the difference Kant sees here, it is one *within* the conduct of rational animals. So far as Kant is talking about (the logic of) action, his Categorical Imperative can be put as a Categorial Declarative (description-rule), i.e., description of what it *is* to act morally: When we (you) act morally, we act in a way we would regard as justified universally, justified no matter who had done it. (This categorial formulation does not tell us how to determine *what was done*; neither does Kant's categorical formulation, although, by speaking of "the" maxim of an action, it pretends to, or anyway makes it seem less problematical than it is.) Perhaps it is by now a little clearer why we are tempted to retort, "But suppose I don't *want* to be moral?"; and also why it would be irrelevant here. The Categorial Declarative does not tell you what you *ought* to do *if* you want to be moral (and hence is untouched by the feeling that no imperative can really be *categorical,* can bind us no matter what); it tells you (part of) what you in fact do when you *are* moral. It cannot—nothing a philosopher says can—insure that you will not act immorally; but it is entirely unaffected by what you do or do not want.

I am not saying that rules do not sometimes sort with imperatives, but only denying that they always do. In the Britannica article (eleventh edition) on chess, only one paragraph of the twenty or so which describe the game is headed "Rules," and only here are we told what we *must* do. This paragraph deals with such matters as the convention of saying "j'adoube" when you touch a piece to straighten it. Is the difference between matters of this kind and the matter of how pieces move, a difference between penalties (which are imposed for misplay) and moves (which are accepted in order to play at all)—so that we would cheerfully say that we can play (are playing) chess without the "j'adoube" convention, but less cheerfully that we can play without following the rule that "the Queen moves in any direction, square or diagonal, whether forward or backward"? This would suggest that we may think of the difference between rule and imperative as one between those actions (or "parts" of actions) which are easy (natural, normal) for us, and those we have to be encouraged to do. (What I do as a rule you may have to be made or directed to do.) We are likely to forget to say "j'adoube," so we have to be *made* (to remember) to do it; but we do not have to be *made* to move the Queen in straight, unobstructed paths.[22] This further suggests that what is thought of as "alienation" is something which occurs *within* moral systems; since these are profoundly haphazard accumulations, it is no surprise that we feel part of some regions of the system and feel apart from other regions.[23]

So the subject of responsibility, of obligation and commitment, opens into the set of questions having to do with differences between doing a thing wrongly or badly (strangely, ineptly, inexactly, partially . . .) and not doing the thing at all. These differences take us into a further region of the concept of an action: we have noted that there are many (specific) ways in which an action can go wrong (at least as many as the myriad excuses we are entitled to proffer when what we have done has resulted in some unhappiness); but it would be incorrect to suppose that we are *obligated* to see to it (to take precautions to insure), *whenever* we undertake to do anything, that none of these ways will come to pass. Our obligation is to avoid doing something at a time and place or in a way which is *likely* to result in some misfortune, or to avoid being careless where it is easy to be, or to be *especially* careful where the action is dangerous or delicate, or avoid the temptation to skip a necessary step when it seems in the moment to make little difference. If

---

[22] Though in another context we might have. Imagine that before chess was introduced into our culture, another game—call it Quest—had been popular with us. In that game, played on a board with 64 squares, and like chess in other respects, the piece called the Damsel had a fickle way of moving: its first move, and every odd move afterwards, followed the rule for the Queen in chess; its even moves followed the rule for the Knight. It may be supposed that when people began to play chess, it often happened that a game had to be stopped upon remembering that several moves earlier a Queen was permitted a Knight's move. The rule for the Queen's move might then have been formulated in some such way as: You must move the Queen in straight, unobstructed paths . . .

[23] Perhaps this difference provides a way of accounting for our tendency sometimes to think of laws as rules and at other times to think of them as commands. This may (in part) depend upon where we—i.e., where our normal actions—stand (or where we imagine them to stand) with respect to the law or system of laws in question. It may also be significant that when you are describing a system of laws, you are likely to think of yourself as external to the system.

for *all* excuses there were relevant obligations, then there would be no excuses and action would become intolerable. Any *particular* excuse may be countered with a *specific* obligation; not even the best excuse will always get you off the hook (That is no excuse; you should have known that was likely to result in an accident, you ought to have paid *particular* heed here, etc.).

Without pretending to give an account of (this part of) obligation, what I think the foregoing considerations indicate is this: a statement of what we *must* do (or say) has point only in the context (against the background) of knowledge that we are in fact doing (or saying) a thing, but doing (saying) it—or running a definite risk of doing or saying it—badly, inappropriately, thoughtlessly, tactlessly, self-defeatingly, etc.; or against the background of knowledge that we are in a certain position or occupy a certain office or station, and are *behaving* or *conducting ourselves* inappropriately, thoughtlessiy, self-defeatingly. . . . The same is true of statements about what we *may* do, as well as those containing other "modal auxiliaries"—e.g., about what we *should* do, or what we *are* or *have* to do, or are *supposed* to do, and about one sense of what we *can* do; these are all intelligible only against the background of what we are doing or are in a position (one sense of "able") to do. These "link verbs" share the linguistic peculiarity that while they are verb-like forms they cannot stand as the main verb of a sentence. This itself would suggest that their use is not one of prescribing some new action to us, but of setting an action which is antecedently relevant to what we are doing or to what we are—setting it relevantly into the larger context of what we are doing or of what we are.[24] "You must (are supposed, obliged, required to) move the Queen in straight paths . . ." or "You may (can, are allowed or permitted to) move the Queen in straight paths . . ." say (assert) no more than "You (do, in fact, always) move the Queen in straight paths . . ."; which of them you say on a given occasion depends not on any special motive or design of yours, nor upon any special mode of argument. There is no question of *going from* "is" to "must," but only of appreciating which of them should be said when, i.e., of appreciating the position or circumstances of the person to whom you are speaking. Whatever makes one of the statements true makes them all true, though not all appropriate.

To tell me what I must do is not the same as to tell me what I ought to do. I must move the Queen in straight paths (in case I am absent-minded and continue moving it like the Damsel; cf. n. 22). What

---

[24] But this requires a great deal of work. We must have a better description of the "class" and the function of "modal auxiliaries," and we need an understanding of what makes something we do "another" action and what makes it "part" of an action in progress.

would it mean to tell me that I *ought* to move the Queen in straight paths? "Ought," unlike "must," implies that there is an alternative; "ought" implies that you can, if you choose, do otherwise. This does *not* mean merely that there is something else to do which is in your *power* ("I *can* move the Queen like the Knight; just watch!") but that there is one within your *rights*. But if I say truly and appropriately, "You must . . ." then in a perfectly good sense nothing you then do can prove me wrong. You CAN *push the little object called the Queen* in many ways, as you can *lift* it or *throw* it across the room; not all of these will be *moving the Queen*. You CAN ask, "Was your action voluntary?" and say to yourself, "All I mean to ask is whether he had a sensation of effort just before he moved," but that will not be finding out whether the action was voluntary. Again, if I have borrowed money then I *must* (under normal circumstances) pay it back (even though it is rather painful).[25] It makes sense to tell me I *ought* to pay it back only if there is a specific reason to suppose, say, that the person from whom I got the money *meant to give* it to me rather than merely *lend* it (nevertheless he needs it badly, worse than I know), or if there is a reason to pay it back tomorrow instead of next week, when the debt falls due (I'll save interest; I'll only spend it and have to make another loan). The difference here resembles that between doing a thing and doing the thing well (thoughtfully, tactfully, sensibly, graciously . . .).

This difference may be made clearer by considering one way principles differ from rules. Rules tell you what to do when you do the thing at all; principles tell you how to do the thing well, with skill or understanding. In competitive games, acting well amounts to doing the sort of thing that will win, so the principles of games recommend strategy. "No raise should [N.B.] be given to partner's suit without at least Q-x-x, J-10-x, K-x-x, A-x-x, or any four trumps. . . ." But you could fail to adopt this and still play bridge, even play well. It is a

---

[25] "Must" retains its logical force here. Kant may not have provided an analysis sufficient to sustain his saying that "a deposit of money must be handed back because if the recipient appropriated it, it would no longer be a deposit"; but Bergson too hastily concludes that Kant's explanation of this in terms of "logical contradiction" is "obviously juggling with words." [See Bergson's *The Two Sources of Morality and Religion* (New York: Holt, Rinehart & Winston, Inc., 1935), p. 77.] The difference between your *depositing* and simply *handing* over some money has in part to do with what you mean or intend to be doing —and with what you *can* mean or intend by doing what you do in the way you do it in that particular historical context. We may, following a suggestion of H. P. Grice's ["Meaning," *The Philosophical Review*, Vol. LXVI (1957)], think of the actions of depositing and of accepting a deposit as complicated "utterances": you intend that what you do shall be understood. Then it will not seem so extraordinary to say that a later "utterance" (viz., appropriating the entrusted money) contradicts a former one (viz., accepting a deposit).

principle of strategy in Culbertson's system ;[26] but another expert may have a different understanding of the game and develop principles of strategy which are equally successful. Principles go with understanding. (Having an understanding of a game is not knowing the rules; you might find a book called Principles of Economics or Psychology, but none called Rules of Economics, etc.) Understanding a principle involves knowing how and where to apply it. But some moves seem so immediately to be called for by the principles of strategy, that their formulations come to be thought of as rules: should we say, "The third hand plays high . . ." or "The third hand should play high . . ."? You may, strictly speaking, be playing bridge if you flout this, but you won't be doing the sort of thing which will win (and therefore not really playing? When is not doing a thing well not really doing the thing?). All players employ maxims (which may be thought of as formulating strategies as though they were moves) in order to facilitate their play; like everything habitual or summary, maxims have their advantages and their dangers. Both the rules which constitute playing the game, and the "rules" or maxims which contribute to playing the game well have their analogues in ordinary moral conduct.

I think it is sometimes felt that drawing an analogy between moral conduct and games makes moral conduct seem misleadingly simple (or trivial?), because there are no rules in moral conduct corresponding to the rules about how the Queen moves in chess.[27] But this misses the point of the analogy, which is that moves and actions have to be done *correctly*; not just any movement you make will be a move, or a promise,

---

[26] Cited in *Hoyle Up-to-Date*, A. H. Morehead and G. Mott-Smith, eds. (New York: Grosset & Dunlap, Inc., 1950).

[27] Some philosophers who employ the notion of a rule have given the impression that there are. What I am suggesting is that even if there aren't, the analogy is still a good one. One of the claims made for the concept of a rule is that it illuminates the notion of justification; and critics of the concept argue that it fails in this and that therefore the concept is unilluminating in the attempt to understand moral conduct. I think both of these claims are improper, resulting in part from the failure to appreciate differences (1) between rules and principles, and (2) between performing an action and making some movements. The concept of rule does illuminate the concept of *action*, but not that of *justified action*. Where there is a question about what I do and I cite a rule in my favor, what I do is to *explain* my action, make clear *what* I was doing, not to justify it, say that what I did was well or rightly done. Where my action is in accord with the relevant rules, it needs no justification. Nor can it receive any: I cannot *justify* moving the Queen in straight, unobstructed paths. See John Rawls' study of this subject, "Two Concepts of Rules," *The Philosophical Review*, Vol. LXIV (1955). My unhappiness with the way in which the analogy is drawn does not diminish my respect for this paper. For a criticism (based, I think, on a misunderstanding) of the view, see H. J. McCloskey, "An Examination of Restricted Utilitarianism," *The Philosophical Review*, Vol. LXVI (1957).

a payment, a request. This does not mean that promising *is* (just) following rules. Yet if someone is tempted not to fulfill a promise, you may say "Promises are kept," or "We keep our promises (that is the sort of thing a promise is)," thus employing a rule-description—what I have called a categorial declarative. You may say "You must keep this promise" (you are underestimating its importance; last time you forgot). This is not the same as "You ought to keep this promise," which is only sensible where you have a reason for breaking it strong enough to allow you to do so without blame (there is a real alternative), but where you are being enjoined to make a *special* effort or sacrifice. [This is partly why "You ought to keep promises" is so queer. It suggests that we not only always want badly to get out of fulfilling promises, but that we always have some good (anyway, *prima facie*) reason for not keeping them (perhaps our own severe discomfort) and that therefore we are acting *well* when we do fulfill. But we aren't, normally; neither well nor ill.] "Ought" is like "must" in requiring a background of action or position into which the action in question is set; and, like "must," it does not form a command, a pure imperative. All of which shows the hopelessness of speaking, in a *general* way, about the "normativeness" of expressions. The Britannica "rules" tell us what we *must* do *in playing* chess, not what we ought to do *if* we want to play. You (must) mean (imply), in speaking English, that something about an action is fishy when you say "The action is voluntary"; you (must) mean, when you ask a person "Ought you to do that?" that there is some *specific* way in which what he is doing might be done more tactfully, carefully, etc. . . . Are these imperatives? Are they categorical or hypothetical? Have you in no way contradicted yourself if you flout them? (Cf. note 25.)

That "modal imperatives" ("must," "supposed to," "are to," "have to" . . .) require the recognition of a background action or position into which the relevant action is placed indicates a portentous difference between these forms of expression and pure imperatives, commands. Whether I can command depends only upon whether I have power or authority, and the only characteristics I must recognize in the object of the command are those which tell me that the object is subject to my power or authority. Employing a modal "imperative," however, requires that I recognize the object as a *person* (someone doing something or in a certain position) to whose reasonableness (reason) I appeal in using the second person. (Compare "Open, Sesame!" with "You must open, Sesame.") This is one reason that commands, pure imperatives, are not paradigms of moral utterance, but represent an alternative to such utterance.

Without pretending that my argument for it has been nearly full or clear enough, let me, by way of summary, flatly state what it is I have

tried to argue about the relation between what you say and what you
(must) mean, i.e., between what you (explicitly) say and what saying
it implies or suggests: If "what A (an utterance) means" is to be
understood in terms of (or even as directly related to) "what is (must
be) meant in (by) saying A," [28] then the meaning of A will not be
given by its analytic or definitional equivalents, nor by its deductive
implications. Intension is not a substitute for intention. Although we
would not call the statement "When we say we know something we
imply (mean) that we have confidence, that we are in a position to
say we know . . ." analytic, yet if the statement is true it is necessarily
true in just this sense: if it is true, then when you ask what the statement supposes you to ask, you (must) mean what the statement says
you (must) mean. Necessary and not analytic: it was—apart from the
parody of Kant—to summarize, and partly explain, this peculiarity that
I called such statements categorial declaratives: declarative, because
something is (authoritatively) made known; categorial, because in
telling us what we (must) mean by asserting that (or questioning
whether) x is F, they tell us what it is for an x to be F (an action to be
moral, a statement claiming knowledge to be a statement expressing
knowledge, a movement to be a move).[29] Shall we say that such statements formulate the rules or the principles of grammar—the moves or
the strategies of talking? [And is this, perhaps, to be thought of as a
difference between grammar and rhetoric? But becoming clearer about
this will require us to see more clearly the difference between not
doing a thing well (here, saying something) and not doing the thing;
and between doing a thing badly and not doing the thing.] The significance of categorial declaratives lies in their teaching or reminding
us that the "pragmatic implications" of our utterances are (or, if we
are feeling perverse, or tempted to speak carelessly, or chafing under
an effort of honesty, let us say *must be*) *meant*; that they are an essential part of what we mean when we say something, of what it is to
mean something. And what we mean (intend) to say, like what we
mean (intend) to do, is something we are responsible for.

---

[28] Such an understanding of meaning is provided in Grice (*op. cit.*), but I do
not think he would be happy about the use I wish to put it to. A conversation
we had was too brief for me to be sure about this, but not too brief for me
to have added, as a result of it, one or two qualifications or clarifications of
what I had said, e.g., the third point of note 31, note 32, and the independent
clause to which the present note is attached.

[29] If truth consists in saying of what is that it is, then (*this* sense or source of)
necessary truth consists in saying of what is *what* it is. The question, "Are these
matters of language or matters of fact?" would betray the obsession I have tried
to calm. I do not claim that this explanation of necessity holds for all statements which seem to us necessary and not analytic, but at best for those whose
topic is actions and which therefore display a rule-description complementarity.

Even with this slight rehabilitation of the notion of normativeness, we can begin to see the special sense in which the philosopher who proceeds from ordinary language is "establishing a norm" in employing his second type of statement. He is certainly not *instituting* norms, nor is he *ascertaining* norms (see note 20); but he may be thought of as *confirming* or *proving* the existence of norms when he reports or describes how we (how to) talk, i.e., when he says (in statements of the second type) what is normative for utterances instanced by statements of the first type. Confirming and proving are other regions of establishing. I have suggested that there are ways normative for instituting and for ascertaining norms; and so are there for confirming or proving or reporting them, i.e., for employing locutions like "We can say . . . ," or "When we say . . . we imply—." The swift use made of them by the philosopher serves to remind mature speakers of a language of something they know; but they would erroneously be employed in trying to report a special usage of one's own, and (not unrelated to this) could not be used to change the meaning of an expression. Since saying something is never *merely* saying something, but is saying something with a certain tune and at a proper cue and while executing the appropriate business, the sounded utterance is only a salience of what is going on when we talk (or the unsounded when we think); so a statement of "what we say" will give us only a feature of what we need to remember. But a native speaker will normally know the rest; learning it was part of learning the language.

Let me warn against two tempting ways to avoid the significance of this. (1) It is perfectly true that English might have developed differently than it has and therefore have imposed different categories on the world than it does; and if so, it would have enabled us to assert, describe, question, define, promise, appeal, etc., in ways other than we do. But using English now—to converse with others in the language, or to understand the world, or to think by ourselves—means knowing which forms in what contexts are normative for performing the activities we perform by using the language. (2) It is no escape to say: "Still I can say what I like; I needn't always use normal forms in saying what I say; I can speak in extraordinary ways, and you will perfectly well understand me." What this calls attention to is the fact that language provides us with ways for (contains forms which are normative for) speaking in special ways, e.g., for changing the meaning of a word, or for speaking, *on particular occasions,* loosely or personally, or paradoxically, cryptically, metaphorically . . . Do you wish to claim that you can speak strangely yet intelligibly—and this of course means intelligibly to yourself as well—in ways not provided in the language for speaking strangely?

It may be felt that I have not yet touched one of Mates' fundamental criticisms. Suppose you grant all that has been said about an ordinary use being normative for what anyone says. Will you still wish to ask: "Does it follow that the ordinary uses which are normative for what professors say are the same as the ordinary uses which are normative for what butchers and bakers say?" Or perhaps: "Is an ordinary use for a professor an *ordinary* ordinary use?" Is that a sensible question?

To determine whether it is, we must appreciate what it is to talk together. The philosopher, understandably, often takes the isolated man bent silently over a book as his model for what using language is. But the primary fact of natural language is that it is something spoken, spoken together. Talking together is acting together, not making motions and noises at one another, nor transferring unspeakable messages or essences from the inside of one closed chamber to the inside of another. The difficulties of talking together are, rather, *real* ones: the activities we engage in by talking are intricate and intricately related to one another. I suppose it will be granted that the professor and the baker can talk together. Consider the most obvious complexities of cooperative activity in which they engage: there is commenting ("Nice day"); commending, persuading, recommending, enumerating, comparing ("The pumpernickel is good, but the whole wheat and the rye even better"); grading, choosing, pointing ("I'll have the darker loaf there"); counting, making change, thanking; warning ("Careful of the step"); promising ("Be back next week") . . . ; all this in addition to the whole nest or combination of actions which comprise the machinery of talking: asserting, referring, conjoining, denying, . . . Now it may be clearer why I wish to say: if the professors and the baker did not understand each other, the professors would not understand one another either.

You may still want to ask: "Does this mean that the professor and baker use particular words like 'voluntary' and 'involuntary,' or 'inadvertently' and 'automatically' the same way? The baker may never have used these words at all." But the question has *now* become, since it is about *specific* expressions, straightforwardly empirical. Here Mates' "two methods" (pp. 69ff.) at last become relevant. But I am at the moment less interested in determining what empirical methods would be appropriate to investigate the matter than I am in posing the following questions: What should we say if it turned out, as it certainly might, that they in fact do use the words differently? Should we, for example, say that therefore we never have a right to say that people use words in the same way without undertaking an empirical investigation; or perhaps say that therefore they speak different languages? What should make us say that they do not speak the same language? Do we really know what it would be like to embark upon an empirical investigation of the *gen-*

eral question whether we (ordinarily, ever) use language the way other people do?

There is too much here to try to unravel. But here are some of the threads: The words "inadvertently" and "automatically," however recondite, are ordinary; there are ordinary contexts (nontechnical, non-political, nonphilosophical contexts) which are normative for their use. It may be that half the speakers of English do not know (or cannot say, which is not the same) what these contexts are. Some native speakers may even use them interchangeably. Suppose the baker is able to convince us that he does. Should we then say: "So the professor has no right to say how '*we* use' 'inadvertently,' or to say that 'when *we* use the one word we say something different from what we say when we use the other' "? Before accepting that conclusion, I should hope that the following consideration would be taken seriously: When "inadvertently" and "automatically" seem to be used indifferently in recounting what someone did, this may not at all show that they are being used synonymously, but only that what each of them says is separately true of the person's action. The decanter is broken and you did it. You may say (and it may be important to consider that you are already embarrassed and flustered) either: "I did it inadvertently" or "I did it automatically." Are you saying the same thing? Well, you automatically *grabbed the cigarette* which had fallen on the table, and inadvertently *knocked over the decanter*. Naming actions is a sensitive occupation.[30] It is easy to overlook the distinction because the two adverbs often go together in describing actions in which a sudden movement results in some mishap.

Suppose the baker does not accept this explanation, but replies: "I use 'automatically' and 'inadvertently' in exactly the same way. I could just as well have said: 'I grabbed the cigarette inadvertently and knocked over the decanter automatically.' " Don't we feel the temptation to reply: "You may *say* this, but you can't say it and describe the same situation; you can't mean what you would mean if you said the other." But suppose the baker insists he can? Will we then be prepared to say: "Well you can't say the one and mean what *I* mean by the other"? Great care would be needed in claiming this, for it may look like I am saying, "I know what I mean and I say they are different." But why is the baker not entitled to this argument? What I must not say is: "I know what words mean in *my* language." Here the argument would have pushed me to madness. It *may* turn out (depending upon just what the dialogue has been and where it was stopped) that we should say to the baker: "If you cooked the way you talk, you would forgo special implements for different jobs, and peel, core, scrape, slice,

---

[30] Austin's work on Excuses provides a way of coming to master this immensely important idea. The way I have put the point here is due directly to it.

carve, chop, and saw, all with one knife. The distinction is there, in the language (as implements are there to be had), and you just impoverish what you say by neglecting it. And there is something you aren't noticing about the world." [31]

But to a philosopher who refuses to acknowledge the distinction we should say something more: not merely that he impoverishes what he can say about actions, but that he is a poor theorist of what it is to do something. The philosopher who asks about everything we do, "Voluntary or not?" has a poor view of action (as the philosopher who asks of everything we say, "True or false?" or "Analytic or synthetic?" has a poor view of communication), in something like the way a man who asks the cook about every piece of food, "Was it cut or not?" has a poor view of preparing food. The cook with only one knife is in much better condition than the philosopher with only "Voluntary or involuntary?" to use in dividing actions, or "True or false?" to use in hacking out meaningful statements. The cook can get on with the preparation of the meal even if he must improvise a method here and there, and makes more of a mess than he would with more appropriate implements. But the philosopher can scarcely *begin* to do his work; there is no job the philosopher has to get on with; nothing ulterior he must do with actions (e.g., explain or predict them), or with statements (e.g., verify them). What he wants to know is what they are, what it is to do something and to say something. To the extent that he improvises a way of getting past the description and division of an action or a statement, or leaves a mess in his account—to that extent he leaves his own job undone. If the philosopher is trying to get clear about what preparing a meal is and asks the cook, "Do you cut the apple or not?," the cook may say, "Watch me!" and then core and peel it. "Watch me!" is what we should reply to the philosopher who asks of our normal, ordinary actions, "Voluntary or not?" and who asks of our ethical and aesthetic judgments, "True or false?" Few speakers of a language utilize the full range of perception which the language provides, just as they do without so

---

[31] Three points about this conclusion need emphasizing. (1) It was reached where the difference concerned isolated *words;* where, that is, the shared *language* was left intact. (2) The tasks to be performed (scraping, chopping, excusing a familiar and not very serious mishap) were such as to allow execution, if more or less crude, with a general or common implement. (3) The question was over the meaning of a word in general, not over its meaning (what it was used to mean) on a particular occasion; there was, I am assuming, no reason to treat the word's use on this occasion as a special one.

Wittgenstein's role in combatting the idea of privacy (whether of the meaning of what is said or of what is done), and in emphasizing the *functions* of language, scarcely needs to be mentioned. It might be worth pointing out that both of these teachings are fundamental to American pragmatism; but then we must keep in mind how different their arguments sound, and admit that in philosophy it is the sound which makes all the difference.

much of the rest of their cultural heritage. Not even the philosopher will come to possess all of his past, but to neglect it deliberately is foolhardy. The consequence of such neglect is that our philosophical memory and perception become fixated upon a few accidents of intellectual history.

I have suggested that the question of "[verifying] an assertion that a given person uses a *word* in a given way or with a given sense" (Mates, *ibid.*, my emphasis) is not the same as verifying assertions that "We say . . ." or that "When we say . . . we imply—." This means that I do not take the "two basic approaches" which Mates offers in the latter part of his paper to be directed to the same question as the one represented in the title he gives to his paper (at least on my interpretation of that question). The questions are designed to elicit different types of information; they are relevant (have point) at different junctures of investigation. Sometimes a question is settled by asking others (or ourselves) what we say here, or whether we ever say such-and-such; on the basis of these data we can make statements like " 'Voluntary' is used of an action only where there is something (real or imagined) fishy about it." I take this to be a "statement about ordinary language" (and equally, about voluntary action). But surely it is not, under ordinary circumstances, an assertion about how a word is used by *me* (or "some given person") ; it is a statement about how the word is used in English. Questions about how a given person is using some *word* can sensibly arise only where there is some specific reason to suppose that he is using the word in an unusual way. This point can be put the other way around : the statement "I (or some given person) use (used) the word X in such-and-such a way" implies (depending on the situation) that you intend (intended) to be using it in a special way, or that someone else is unthinkingly misusing it, or using it misleadingly, and so on. This is another instance of the principle that actions which are normal will not tolerate any special description. In a *particular* case you may realize that words are not to be taken normally, that some want or fear or special intention of the speaker is causing an aberration in the drift of his words. A little girl who says to her brother, "You can have half my candy" may mean, "Don't take any!" ; the husband who screams in fury, "Still no buttons!" may really be saying, "If I were honest, I'd do what Gauguin did." A knave or a critic or an heiress may say, "X is good" and mean "I want or expect or command you to like (or approve of) X"; and we, even without a special burden of malice, or of taste, or of money, may sometimes find ourselves imitating them.

Mates interprets Ryle's assertion that the ordinary use of "voluntary" applies to actions which are disapproved to mean that "the ordinary man applies the word only to actions of which he disapproves" (p. 72) ;

this apparently involves a reference to that man's personal "aims, feeling, beliefs, and hopes"; and these, in turn, are supposedly part merely of the pragmatics (not the semantics) of a word. It is therefore a mistake, Mates concludes, to claim that the philosopher is using the word in a "stretched, extraordinary *sense*" (*ibid., my emphasis*) merely on the ground that he may not happen to feel disapproving about an action he calls voluntary. The mistake, however, is to suppose that the ordinary use of a word is a function of the internal state of the speaker. (It is sometimes to emphasize that your remarks about "use" are not remarks about such states that you want to say you are talking about the *logic* of ordinary language.) Another reason for the tenacity of the idea that a statement of what we mean when we say so-and-so (a statement of the second type) must be synthetic is that we suppose it to be *describing* the mental processes of the person talking. To gain perspective on that idea, it may be of help to consider that instead of saying to the child who said he *knew* (when we knew he had no right to say so), "You mean you *think* so," we might have said, "You *don't* know (or, That is not what it is to know something); you just think so." This says neither more nor less than the formulation about what he *means,* and neither of them is a description of what is going on inside the child. They are both statements which teach him what he has a *right* to say, what knowledge is.

Mates tells us (*ibid.*) that his "intensional approach" is meant, in part, "to do justice to the notions (1) that what an individual means by a word depends at least in part upon what he wants to mean by that word, and (2) that he may have to think awhile before he discovers what he 'really' means by a given word." With respect to the first notion, I should urge that we do justice to the fact that an individual's intentions or wishes can no more produce the general meaning for a word than they can produce horses for beggars, or home runs from pop flies, or successful poems out of unsuccessful poems.[32] This may be made clearer by noticing, with respect to the second notion, that often when an individual is thinking "what he 'really' means" (in the sense of having second thoughts about something), he is not thinking what he really means by a given *word*. You have second thoughts in such cases just because you cannot make words mean what you wish (*by* wishing); it is for that reason that what you say on a given occasion may not be

---

[32] I am not, of course, denying that what you *say* depends upon what you intend to be saying. I am, rather, denying that intending is to be understood as a wanting or wishing. And I am suggesting that you could not mean one thing rather than another ($=$ you could not mean anything) by a given word on a given occasion without relying on a (general) meaning of that word which is independent of your intention on that occasion (unless what you are doing is *giving* the word a special meaning). For an analysis of meaning in terms of intention, see Grice, *op. cit.*

what you really mean. To say what you really mean you will have to say something different, change the words; or, as a special case of this, change the meaning of a word. Changing the meaning is not wishing it were different. This is further confirmed by comparing the locutions "X means YZ" and "I mean by X, YZ." The former holds or fails to hold, whatever I wish to mean. And the latter, where meaning does depend on me, is performative;[33] something I am doing to the word X, not something I am wishing about it.

What these remarks come to is this: it is not clear what such an activity as my-finding-out-what-I-mean-by-a-word would be. But there obviously is finding-out-what-a-word-means. You do this by consulting a dictionary or a native speaker who happens to know. There is also something we may call finding-out-what-a-word-really-means. This is done when you already know what the dictionary can teach you; when, for some reason or other, you are forced into philosophizing. Then you begin by recollecting the various things we should say were such-and-such the case. Socrates gets his antagonists to withdraw their definitions not because they do not know what their words mean, but because they do know what they (their words) mean, and therefore know that Socrates has led them into paradox. (How could I be led into a paradox if I could mean what I wished by my words? Because I must be consistent? But how could I *be inconsistent* if words would mean what I wanted them to mean?) What they had not realized was what they were saying, or, what they were *really* saying, and so not known *what they meant.* To this extent, they had not known themselves, and not known the world. I mean, of course, the ordinary world. That may not be all there is, but it is important enough: morality is in that world, and so are force and love; so is art and a part of knowledge (the part which is about that world); and so is religion (wherever God is). Some mathematics and science, no doubt, are not. This is why you will not find out what "number" or "neurosis" or "mass" or "mass society" mean if you only listen for our ordinary uses of these terms.[34] But you will never find out what voluntary action is if you fail to see when we should say of an action that it is voluntary.

One may still feel the need to say: "Some actions *are* voluntary and some are involuntary. It would be convenient (for what?) to call all actions voluntary which are not involuntary. Surely I can call them

---

[33] Or else it is a *special* report, like the one on p. 107, lines 25f.; but it is still not a description of my wishes or intentions. The best place to find out what a "performative" is is Austin's *How to Do Things with Words* (Cambridge, Mass.: Harvard University Press, 1962). See also "Other Minds," *Logic and Language,* 2nd series, pp. 142ff.

[34] This may be summarized by saying that there is no such thing as *finding out* what a number, etc., is. This would then provide the occasion and the justification for logical construction.

anything I like? Surely what I *call* them doesn't affect what they *are*?"
Now: how will you tell me what "they" are? [35] What we need to ask
ourselves here is: In what sort of situations does it make no difference
what I call a thing? or: At what point in a dialogue does it become
natural or proper for me to say, "I (you) can call it what I (you)
like"? At this point it may be safe to say that the question is (has
become) verbal.[36] If you really have a way of telling just what is de-
noted by "all actions which are not involuntary," then you can call
them anything you like.

I just tried to characterize the situation in which we ordinarily ask,
"What does X mean?" and to characterize the *different* situation in
which we ask, "What does X really mean?" These questions neither
conflict nor substitute for one another, though philosophers often take
the second as a profound version of the first—perhaps to console themselves for their lack of progress. Isn't this part of the trouble about
synonymy? "Does X *really* mean the same as Y?" is not a profound
version of "Does X mean the same as Y?" It (its occasion) is, though
related to the first in obvious and devious ways, different. The same
goes for the pair: "What did he do?" and "What did he really (literally) *do*?"; and for the pair: "What do you see?" and "What do you
really (immediately) *see*?"; and for the pair: "Is the table solid?" and
"Is the table *really* (absolutely) solid?" Since the members of the pairs
are *obviously* different, philosophers who do not see that the difference
in the second members lies in their occasions, in where and when they
are posed, handsomely provide special entities, new worlds, for them
to be about. But this can only perpetrate—it will not penetrate—a new
reality.

The profoundest as well as the most superficial questions can be
understood only when they have been placed in their natural environ-
ments. (What makes a statement or a question profound is not its
placing but its timing.) The philosopher is no more magically equipped
to remove a question from its natural environment than he is to remove
himself from any of the conditions of intelligible discourse. Or rather,
he may remove himself, but his mind will not follow. This, I hope it
is clear, does not mean that the philosopher will not eventually come
to distinctions, and use words to mark them, at places and in ways

---

[35] Cf, D. F. Pears, "Incompatibilities of Colours," *Logic and Language,* 2nd
series, p. 119, n. 2.

[36] One of the best ways to get past the idea that philosophy's concern with
language is a concern with words (with "verbal" matters) is to read Wisdom.
Fortunately it is a pleasant way; because since the idea is one that you have
to get past again and again, the way past it will have to be taken again and
again.

which depart from the currently ordinary lines of thought.[37] But it does suggest that (and why) when his recommendations come too fast, with too little attention to the particular problem for which we have gone to him, we feel that instead of thoughtful advice we have been handed a form letter. Attention to the details of cases as they arise may not provide a quick path to an all-embracing system; but at least it promises genuine instead of spurious clarity.

Some philosophers will find this program too confining. Philosophy, they will feel, was not always in such straits; and it will be difficult for them to believe that the world and the mind have so terribly altered that philosophy must relinquish old excitements to science and to poetry. There, it may be claimed, new uses are still invented by profession, and while this makes the scientist and the poet harder to understand initially, it enables them eventually to renew and to deepen and to articulate our understanding. No wonder the philosopher will gape at such band wagons. But he must sit still. Both because, where he does not wish to invent (hopes not to invent), he is not entitled to the rewards and licenses of those who do; and because he would otherwise be running from his peculiar task—one which has become homelier perhaps, but still quite indispensable to the mind. The "unwelcome consequences" (Mates, p. 67) which may attend using words in ways which are (have become) privately extraordinary is just that our understanding should lose its grasp. Not only is it true that this can happen without our being aware of it, it is often very difficult to become aware of it—like becoming aware that we have grown pedantic or childish or slow. The meaning of words *will*, of course, stretch and shrink, and they will be stretched and be shrunk. One of the great responsibilities of the philosopher lies in appreciating the natural and the normative ways in which such things happen, so that he may make us aware of the one and capable of evaluating the other. It is a wonderful step towards understanding the abutment of language and the world when we see it to be a matter of convention. But this idea, like every other, endangers as it releases the imagination. For some will then suppose that a private meaning is not more arbitrary than one arrived at publicly, and that since language inevitably changes, there is no reason not to change it arbitrarily. Here we need to remind ourselves that ordinary language is natural language, and that its changing is natural. (It is unfortunate that artificial language has come to seem a general *alternative* to natural language;[38] it

---

[37] As Austin explicitly says. See above, p. 49.

[38] This sometimes appears to be the only substantive agreement between the philosophers who proceed from ordinary language and those who proceed by constructing artificial languages. But this may well be obscuring their deeper disagreements, which are, I believe, less about language than about whether the time has come to drag free of the philosophical tradition established in

would, I suggest, be better thought of as one of its capacities.) Some philosophers, apparently, suppose that because natural language is "constantly" changing it is too unstable to support one exact thought, let alone a clear philosophy. But this Heraclitean anxiety is unnecessary: linguistic change is itself an object of respectable study. And it misses the significance of that change. It is exactly because the language which contains a culture changes with the changes of that culture that philosophical awareness of ordinary language is illuminating; it is that which explains how the language we traverse every day can contain undiscovered treasure. To see that ordinary language is natural is to see that (perhaps even see why) it is normative for what can be said. And also to see how it is by searching definitions that Socrates can coax the mind down from self-assertion—subjective assertion and private definition—and lead it back, through the community, home. That this also renews and deepens and articulates our understanding tells us something about the mind, and provides the consolation of philosophers.

Professor Mates, at one point in his paper, puts his doubts about the significance of the claims of ordinary language this way: "Surely the point is not merely that if you use the word 'voluntary' just as the philosopher does, you may find yourself entangled in the philosophic problem of the Freedom of the Will" (p. 67). Perhaps the reason he thinks this a negligible consequence is that he hears it on analogy with the assertion, "If you use the term 'space-time' just as the physicist does, you may find yourself entangled in the philosophic problem of simultaneity." The implication is that the problem must simply be faced, not avoided. I, however, hear the remark differently: If you use alcohol just as the alcoholic does, or pleasure as the neurotic does, you may find yourself entangled in the practical problem of the freedom of the will.

---

response to, and as part of, the "scientific revolution" of the sixteenth and seventeenth centuries. I have found instruction about this in conversations with my friend and colleague Thomas S. Kuhn, to whom I am also indebted for having read (and forced the rewriting of) two shorter versions of this paper.

SELECTED

BIBLIOGRAPHY

The main forbears of so-called ordinary language philosophy are Moore and Wittgenstein; its main practitioners have been the immediate followers of Wittgenstein and a group of Oxford philosophers led by Ryle and Austin. In addition to works of these philosophers, the following list includes some general surveys of recent British philosophy and a few further works on the particular issues treated in the essays contained in this volume. Altogether, this list represents only a small sample of the works on and in ordinary language philosophy which have appeared in recent years and which have filled such journals as *Mind, Analysis,* the *Philosophical Review,* and the *Proceedings of the Aristotelian Society.* More complete lists can be found in Anthony Quinton, "Linguistic Analysis," *Philosophy in the Mid-Century,* Raymond Klibansky, ed. (Florence: La Nuova Italia Editrice, 1958), Vol. II, pp. 146-202, and in *Logical Positivism,* A. J. Ayer, ed. (New York: Free Press of Glencoe, Inc., 1959), pp. 381-446.

MOORE AND WITTGENSTEIN

Moore, G. E., *Philosophical Papers.* London: George Allen & Unwin, 1959.
———, *Philosophical Studies.* London: Routledge & Kegan Paul, Ltd., 1922.

Wittgenstein, Ludwig, *The Blue and Brown Books.* Oxford: Basil
Blackwell & Mott, Ltd., 1958.
——, *Philosophical Investigations.* Oxford: Basil Blackwell & Mott,
Ltd., 1953.

FOLLOWERS OF WITTGENSTEIN

Lazerowitz, Morris, *The Structure of Metaphysics.* London: Routledge
& Kegan Paul, Ltd., 1955.
Malcolm, Norman, *Dreaming.* London: Routledge & Kegan Paul, Ltd.,
1959.
——, *Knowledge and Certainty.* Englewood Cliffs, N.J.: Prentice-
Hall, Inc., 1963.
Waismann, Friedrich, "Analytic-Synthetic," *Analysis,* Vol. X (1949-
1950), 25-40; Vol. XI (1950-1951), 25-38, 49-61, 115-24; Vol.
XIII (1952-1953), 1-14, 73-89.
Wisdom, John, *Philosophy and Psycho-Analysis.* Oxford: Basil Black-
well & Mott, Ltd., 1953.

OXFORD PHILOSOPHERS

Austin, J. L., *How to Do Things with Words.* Cambridge, Mass.:
Harvard University Press, 1962.
——, *Philosophical Papers.* Oxford: The Clarendon Press, 1961.
——, *Sense and Sensibilia.* Oxford: The Clarendon Press, 1962.
Flew, Antony, ed., *Essays in Conceptual Analysis.* London: Macmillan
& Co., Ltd., 1956.
——, ed., *Logic and Language,* 1st series. Oxford: Basil Blackwell
& Mott, Ltd., 1951.
——, ed., *Logic and Language,* 2nd series. Oxford: Basil Blackwell
& Mott, Ltd., 1953.
Hampshire, Stuart, *Thought and Action.* London: Chatto & Windus,
Ltd., 1959.
Ryle, Gilbert, *The Concept of Mind.* London: Hutchinson & Co., Ltd.,
1949.
——, *Dilemmas.* London: Cambridge University Press, 1954.
——, *Philosophical Arguments.* Oxford: The Clarendon Press, 1945.
Strawson, P. F., *Individuals.* London: Methuen & Co., Ltd., 1959.

GENERAL SURVEYS

Ayer, A. J., *et al., The Revolution in Philosophy.* London: Macmillan
& Co., Ltd., 1956.

Urmson, J. O., *Philosophical Analysis*. Oxford: The Clarendon Press, 1956.

Warnock, G. J., *English Philosophy since 1900*. London: Oxford University Press, 1958.

FURTHER WORKS ON ORDINARY LANGUAGE

Baier, Kurt, "The Ordinary Use of Words," *Proceedings of the Aristotelian Society,* Vol. LII (1951-1952), 47-70.

Campbell, C. A., "Common-Sense Propositions and Philosophical Paradoxes," *Proceedings of the Aristotelian Society,* Vol. XLV (1944-1945), 1-25.

Chappell, V. C., "Malcolm on Moore," *Mind,* Vol. LXX (1961), 417-425.

Chisholm, Roderick M., "Philosophers and Ordinary Language," *Philosophical Review,* Vol. LX (1951), 317-328.

Fodor, Jerry A. and Jerrold J. Katz, "The Availability of What We Say," *Philosophical Review,* Vol. LXXII (1963), 57-71.

Grant, C. K., "Polar Concepts and Metaphysical Arguments," *Proceedings of the Aristotelian Society,* Vol. LVI (1955-1956), 83-108.

Henson, Richard G., *Philosophy and the Ordinary Uses of Words*. Ph.D. dissertation, Yale University, 1957; to be published in 1964.

Katz, Jerrold J. and Jerry A. Fodor, "What's Wrong with the Philosophy of Language?" *Inquiry,* Vol. V (1962), 197-237.

Malcolm, Norman, "Philosophy and Ordinary Language," *Philosophical Review,* Vol. LX (1951), 329-340.

Passmore, John, "Professor Ryle's Use of 'Use' and 'Usage,' " *Philosophical Review,* Vol. LXIII (1954), 58-64.

Putnam, H., "Dreaming and 'Depth Grammar,' " *Analytical Philosophy,* R. J. Butler, ed. Oxford: Basil Blackwell & Mott, Ltd., 1962, pp. 211-235.

Watkins, J. W. N., *et al.,* Discussion of the Paradigm Case Argument, *Analysis,* Vol. XVIII (1957-1958), 25-42, 94-96, 117-120, 150-152.

Ziff, Paul, *Semantic Analysis*. Ithaca, N.Y.: Cornell University Press. 1960.

A CATALOGUE OF
SELECTED DOVER BOOKS
IN ALL FIELDS OF INTEREST

A CATALOGUE OF SELECTED DOVER
BOOKS IN ALL FIELDS OF INTEREST

CELESTIAL OBJECTS FOR COMMON TELESCOPES, T. W. Webb. The most used book in amateur astronomy: inestimable aid for locating and identifying nearly 4,000 celestial objects. Edited, updated by Margaret W. Mayall. 77 illustrations. Total of 645pp. 5⅜ x 8½.
20917-2, 20918-0 Pa., Two-vol. set $8.00

HISTORICAL STUDIES IN THE LANGUAGE OF CHEMISTRY, M. P. Crosland. The important part language has played in the development of chemistry from the symbolism of alchemy to the adoption of systematic nomenclature in 1892. ". . . wholeheartedly recommended,"—Science. 15 illustrations. 416pp. of text. 5⅝ x 8¼.
63702-6 Pa. $6.00

BURNHAM'S CELESTIAL HANDBOOK, Robert Burnham, Jr. Thorough, readable guide to the stars beyond our solar system. Exhaustive treatment, fully illustrated. Breakdown is alphabetical by constellation: Andromeda to Cetus in Vol. 1; Chamaeleon to Orion in Vol. 2; and Pavo to Vulpecula in Vol. 3. Hundreds of illustrations. Total of about 2000pp. 6⅛ x 9¼.
23567-X, 23568-8, 23673-0 Pa., Three-vol. set $26.85

THEORY OF WING SECTIONS: INCLUDING A SUMMARY OF AIR-FOIL DATA, Ira H. Abbott and A. E. von Doenhoff. Concise compilation of subatomic aerodynamic characteristics of modern NASA wing sections, plus description of theory. 350pp. of tables. 693pp. 5⅜ x 8½.
60586-8 Pa. $6.50

DE RE METALLICA, Georgius Agricola. Translated by Herbert C. Hoover and Lou II. Hoover. The famous Hoover translation of greatest treatise on technological chemistry, engineering, geology, mining of early modern times (1556). All 289 original woodcuts. 638pp. 6¾ x 11.
60006-8 Clothbd. $17.50

THE ORIGIN OF CONTINENTS AND OCEANS, Alfred Wegener. One of the most influential, most controversial books in science, the classic statement for continental drift. Full 1966 translation of Wegener's final (1929) version. 64 illustrations. 246pp. 5⅜ x 8½.   61708-4 Pa. $3.00

THE PRINCIPLES OF PSYCHOLOGY, William James. Famous long course complete, unabridged. Stream of thought, time perception, memory, experimental methods; great work decades ahead of its time. Still valid, useful; read in many classes. 94 figures. Total of 1391pp. 5⅜ x 8½.
20381-6, 20382-4 Pa., Two-vol. set $13.00

AMERICAN ANTIQUE FURNITURE, Edgar G. Miller, Jr. The basic coverage of all American furniture before 1840: chapters per item chronologically cover all types of furniture, with more than 2100 photos. Total of 1106pp. 7⅞ x 10¾.   21599-7, 21600-4 Pa., Two-vol. set $17.90

ILLUSTRATED GUIDE TO SHAKER FURNITURE, Robert Meader. Director, Shaker Museum, Old Chatham, presents up-to-date coverage of all furniture and appurtenances, with much on local styles not available elsewhere. 235 photos. 146pp. 9 x 12.   22819-3 Pa. $5.00

ORIENTAL RUGS, ANTIQUE AND MODERN, Walter A. Hawley. Persia, Turkey, Caucasus, Central Asia, China, other traditions. Best general survey of all aspects: styles and periods, manufacture, uses, symbols and their interpretation, and identification. 96 illustrations, 11 in color. 320pp. 6⅛ x 9¼.   22366-3 Pa. $6.00

CHINESE POTTERY AND PORCELAIN, R. L. Hobson. Detailed descriptions and analyses by former Keeper of the Department of Oriental Antiquities and Ethnography at the British Museum. Covers hundreds of pieces from primitive times to 1915. Still the standard text for most periods. 136 plates, 40 in full color. Total of 750pp. 5⅜ x 8½.
23253-0 Pa. $10.00

THE WARES OF THE MING DYNASTY, R. L. Hobson. Foremost scholar examines and illustrates many varieties of Ming (1368-1644). Famous blue and white, polychrome, lesser-known styles and shapes. 117 illustrations, 9 full color, of outstanding pieces. Total of 263pp. 6⅛ x 9¼. (Available in U.S. only)   23652-8 Pa. $6.00

ACKERMANN'S COSTUME PLATES, Rudolph Ackermann. Selection of 96 plates from the *Repository of Arts*, best published source of costume for English fashion during the early 19th century. 12 plates also in color. Captions, glossary and introduction by editor Stella Blum. Total of 120pp. 8⅜ x 11¼.   23690-0 Pa. $4.50

Prices subject to change without notice.

Available at your book dealer or write for free catalogue to Dept. GI, Dover Publications, Inc., 180 Varick St., N.Y., N.Y. 10014. Dover publishes more than 175 books each year on science, elementary and advanced mathematics, biology, music, art, literary history, social sciences and other areas.